D1624012

Close to My Heart

DOROTHY STERLING

Close to My Heart

An Autobiography

The Quantuck Lane Press

NEW YORK

Close To My Heart: An Autobiography
Dorothy Sterling

The text and display type of this book are set in Cochin
Composition and book design by Rubina Yeh
Manufacturing by: Maple-Vail Book Manufacturing Group

Library of Congress Cataloging-in-Publication Data

Sterling, Dorothy, 1913-
  Close to my heart : an autobiography / Dorothy Sterling. — 1st ed.
     p. cm.
   ISBN 1-59372-004-1
  1. Sterling, Dorothy, 1913- 2. Authors, American — 20th century — Biography.
3. Jewish women — United States — Biography. 4. Journalists — United States —
Biography. 5. Historians — United States — Biography. 6. African Americans —
Historiography. I. Title.

  PS3569.T3877Z465 2004
  808'.0092 — dc22

                          2004012429

The Quantuck Lane Press, New York
Distributed by: W.W. Norton & Company, 500 Fifth Avenue, New York, NY
10110
www.wwnorton.com
W.W. Norton & Company Ltd., Castle House, 75/76 Wells Street, London, WIT
3QT

1 2 3 4 5 6 7 8 9 0

CONTENTS

Close to My Heart

CHAPTER

1

Washington Heights, where I was born in 1913, was a quiet residential neighborhood between the Hudson and Harlem rivers, predominantly Jewish around Fort Washington Avenue and Riverside Drive, with Irish and Italians near the Polo Grounds, then New York's newest baseball stadium. Although apartment buildings lined the streets and a subway carried workers to jobs in lower Manhattan, the area had a small-town feeling. Automobiles were scarce; deliveries were made by horse-drawn wagons, and boys played stickball in the streets. From tree-covered Riverside Park one could watch ferryboats crossing the Hudson River to New Jersey. A lighthouse at the river's edge was a favorite picnic place.

We lived at 65 Fort Washington Avenue, a six-story walkup at the corner of 161st Street. My parents, Joseph and Elsie Dannenberg, were second-generation Jewish Americans whose grandparents had emigrated from Germany in the decade before the Civil War. Dad, the first member of his family to go to college, was a lawyer, earning $30 a week in a firm on

1

Rector Street, at the southern tip of Manhattan. Mother had graduated from normal school and taught for a year but was now a housewife intent on raising a family.

My father's brother, Manny, and his family—Aunt Alma, Edgar, and Caryl—lived around the corner near Riverside Drive; his parents, Moses and Celia Dannenberg, were across the street on Fort Washington Avenue. Every morning before going to his dry goods store in Harlem, Grandpa stopped in to greet us. A snappy dresser who wore a derby hat and a flower in his buttonhole, he was, like most small shopkeepers, a member of Tammany Hall, the political machine that controlled the city. At club meetings his Irish colleagues called him "Mike."

On sunny Sundays, Grandpa walked Edgar, two years my senior, and me up Fort Washington Avenue to 168th Street, where a deaf and dumb asylum, as it was then called, was located. Boys in slate-blue uniforms marched and wheeled smartly to the rhythm of a band and we thought we were watching a parade. Catty-corner across the street were rocky, scrub-covered acres which we called "our mountain." Today the Columbia Presbyterian Medical Center sprawls over "our mountain" and the deaf and dumb asylum is a parking garage.

Grandma Celia, who wore floor-length black dresses and high-buttoned shoes, never went out walking, but she took us to our first movies. In the little Costello Theatre two blocks from home we saw Charlie Chaplin in *The Kid* and, in the last year of World War I, hissed the German kaiser in the newsreels, chanting along with the rest of the youthful audience, "Down by the river, Down by the lake, the Kaiser's got a bellyache."

The sidewalk in front of our apartment house was the children's playground. Mothers sat on camp chairs, rocking baby carriages and keeping an eye on toddlers on tricycles. While the older girls jumped rope or played hopscotch, I trailed cousin Edgar and the boys who were shooting marbles in the gutter. All games stopped when the ice wagon arrived and the driver gave us slivers of ice to suck before he made his deliveries. Occasionally an organ grinder and monkey appeared and, captivated by the monkey's antics, we begged for pennies to put in his cup. Once or twice a year a merry-go-round mounted on the bed of a wagon announced itself with tinny music and there were more frantic pleas for pennies.

The courtyard of the apartment house also provided daily drama as peddlers hawked their wares, straining their lungs to announce their presence. The scissors grinder with his grinding wheel on his back came weekly, and the old-clothes dealer with his stentorian call "I CASH CLOTHES" sent housewives racing down the stairs with armloads of old suits. We

3

must have been more prosperous than our neighbors, because Mother did not sell our old clothes, but gave them away to needy individuals. I remember with discomfort a visit from a recipient of her largesse—a shabby little woman with the smell of poverty about her. In heavily accented English, she thanked my mother too profusely for our castoffs, then kissed her hand. Mother acknowledged the tribute with advice on thrift and cleanliness.

From my earliest years, Mother and I did not see eye to eye. She liked neatness; "A place for everything and everything in its place" was one of her oft-repeated mottoes. I got spots on my dresses, scuffed my shoes, and scattered belongings around. I was not interested in dolls and longed for a Lionel train set like Edgar's. But our main struggle began with my hair. I was a blonde, blue-eyed child born to brown-haired parents. Blonde was a plus. Gentlemen preferred blondes even in 1913. Blonde, yes. But kinky? Mother, who in her high school yearbook had been voted as having the "most beautiful hair," dreamed of Mary Pickford curls and pink ribbon bows for me. No matter how hard she brushed—and she brushed hard—the corkscrew curls she constructed quickly reverted to tight little waves. So she brushed again, while I squirmed and screamed and danced out of reach. Later she tried hot olive oil shampoos until I smelled like a salad bowl.

Close to My Heart

The battle between my mother and my hair continued until I was old enough to go to a beauty parlor. Then Mr. Maurice or Mr. Charles or Mr. Jean would douse my head in sticky lotions, set the hair in wide waves and place me under a dryer. No use. A day later it had returned to its unfashionable tight waves. Even when I was in my forties I still made weekly trips to the beauty parlor. I was not liberated until the 1960s, when black women like Angela Davis and Kathleen Cleaver appeared with their stunning Afros. Then my niece, whose hair was almost as recalcitrant as mine, introduced me to the Jewfro. No more hairbrush, no more oils and lotions—only an Afro comb to fluff out the curls. Free at last!

The struggle with my hair was the worst moment of the morning, but getting dressed in 1916 or so was a trying business for girls. My clothes consisted of a bodice that buttoned in the back, bloomers that buttoned to the bodice, then stockings that fastened to the bloomers. Over this went a slip and a dress, with more back buttons. As if this wasn't enough, we wore high-buttoned shoes, which had to be fastened with a button hook. Impatient, eager to be independent, I hated the routine of dressing, which increased my dependency and brought on more clashes with my mother.

My parents were good, kind people who longed to bring me up properly. They were not child abusers. They spanked me occasionally, slapped when goaded beyond endurance, but they were young—twenty-two and twenty-five—when I was born, and they had no books on child psychology to guide them. They were genuinely perplexed when their willful, frizzy-haired daughter planted her feet firmly and announced, almost as soon as she could string words together, "I won't be made to do things." Unable to cope with my tantrums, they did something unusual for their circle and time. They took me to a child psychologist—"alienist," he was called then. I cannot recall the sessions, but family legend reported his advice: "Curb her will, but do not break it." Perhaps this brought me some freedom to grow up in my own way, although it never completely bridged the gap between Mother's way and my own.

After my sister Alice was born in 1916, I was sent off to kindergarten. There was no messy clay or finger paints in Mrs. Lapham's apartment on Riverside Drive. We drew with crayons, filling in coloring books and trying to stay within the lines, and made paste by mixing flour and water. With sticky fingers and blunt scissors we then cut colored paper to make chains. Some were hung on the kindergarten walls; others were brought home to decorate our Christmas trees.

Christmas trees? Most of the children in Mrs. Lapham's kindergarten were Jewish, but on December 25th we had fragrant fir trees in our living rooms with presents from Santa Claus piled up on the floor. What's more, a few months later Easter bunnies delivered baskets filled with jelly beans and colored eggs. I never heard of Chanukah and knew of Rosh Hashanah and Yom Kippur only as days when my father stayed home from work. We had no Seder at Passover, although Mother made delicious dishes with matzoth, sprinkling them with butter and sugar or crumbling them to make pancakes.

I did not hear the word "Jew" until I was five or six and our family and Uncle Manny's were having a picnic in the country. We were sitting under a tree eating sandwiches and drinking lemonade from paper cups when some farm children drew near and shouted, "Dirty Jews! Dirty Jews! Kikes!" I knew something unpleasant was happening, but the grownups, refusing to explain, quietly shepherded us back to the car. Recently I checked with friends from those days — there aren't many of us left — and found that they had similar experiences. "I didn't know I was Jewish," one wrote, "until my cousin and I were playing one day, jumping off the steps of Grant's Tomb. Some other little girls (perhaps aged seven to my five) said we had 'no right' to play there because we were Jews." Others recalled that their parents went to temple on the High Holy Days — "twice-a-year Jews," they were nicknamed — but observed no rituals or dietary laws.

Nor did my parents or grandparents ever mention their German background. Mother baked schnecken rather than cinnamon buns and said "Gesundheit" when we sneezed, but the only German sentence we heard was "Nicht für Kinder," and Alice and I quickly learned what that meant. Keeping silent about their background was doubtless part of the desire of immigrants to assimilate. But it also must have been heightened during World War I, when a wave of anti-German sentiment swept the country — when sauerkraut became liberty cabbage and dachshunds were stoned in the streets. Some German-Americans anglicized their names, but most, like my parents, were content to stress their 100 percent Americanism and shy away from pacifists or conscientious objectors.

Shortly before my fifth birthday I was walking on Broadway with Mother when an army of newsboys raced out of the subway kiosk at 157th Street shouting, "EXTRA! EXTRA! THE WAR IS OVER! READ ALL ABOUT IT!" By then I was able to make a stab at reading about it. The *New York Times* was delivered to our door every morning, along with bottles of milk and cream. It was my father's chief authority. Anything that important to him became important to me. By persistent questioning I deciphered the words in the box, then upper right, on the paper's front page: ALL THE NEWS THAT'S FIT TO PRINT. Like the Rosetta stone, these words led me to others and I was soon off and running.

Close to My Heart

Our home was not exactly a cultural oasis. In the year of my birth, modernism had been introduced to America at the International Exhibition of Modern Art in the Armory at Lexington Avenue and 25th Street. There New Yorkers got their first glimpse of paintings by Picasso, Matisse, Cézanne, and Marcel Duchamp, whose "Nude Descending a Staircase" was the most talked-of picture in the show. Dad undoubtedly agreed with the *New York Times*'s opinion that the show was "part of the general movement to disrupt, degrade, if not destroy, not only art but literature and society too. The Cubists and Futurists are cousins to anarchists in politics." The only paintings on our living-room walls were reproductions of Rosa Bonheur's "Horse Fair" and Millet's "Angelus."

There were few books also until I began to read the standard children's fare: Bunny Brown and his Sister Sue, the Bobbsey twins, and Tom Swift, that first hero of science fiction, who drove cars, flew planes, and traversed the ocean bottom in a submarine. These soft-covered books, which were handed from boy to boy and were smudged and torn when they reached me, carried me far from Fort Washington Avenue to a world where young people were foiling villains and having hair-raising adventures.

Pleased by my precocity, Mother paid little attention to the content of my books, although she soon objected, in a phrase repeated throughout my youth, to having me "lying around the house all day reading." Perforce, I must go outdoors, exercise, make friends. Dispatched downstairs, I usually managed to smuggle along a book. If I huddled against the wall of the building, she wouldn't see me reading when she looked out of the window. By then I felt too old to squat alongside Edgar and his friends, nor would they always tolerate me. Sometimes I joined the girls, bouncing a ball to "One-two-three-O'Leary," or hopped from one chalked-off square to another to pick up the potsy in our version of hopscotch. But I was awkward at jumping rope and, fearing to make a fool of myself, rarely tried to improve my performance. In winter I enjoyed bellywhopping, steering my Flexible Flyer down the steep hill to Riverside Park. But I never learned to ice skate or ride a bike. My happiest moments outdoors were spent on "our mountain" as Edgar and I clambered up the rocks, exploring a stream where a water snake lived and finding, almost at the summit, the remains of the fort built by General Washington during the American Revolution. There, in niches that must have been gun emplacements, we ate our jelly sandwiches—peanut butter was not yet the food of choice of the young—and looked across the Hudson to the Palisades.

As Edgar became increasingly preoccupied with boys' activities, I went alone to Riverside Park, where I discovered dandelions and blue and white violets.

Enchanted by the violets, I picked a little bunch; then, standing on the curb, tried to sell it to passing motorists. I can only explain this strange behavior by recalling the importance of money in our household. The expansion of the American economy during the war, when the United States supplied the Allied powers with guns and grain, had continued afterward, and prosperity had trickled down to my parents and their friends. Uncle Manny's business, selling silk linings to furriers, was far more profitable than anything Grandpa had dreamed of; Dad's law practice picked up, too, although at a slower rate. Mother was able to hire a "green girl," a Polish or Hungarian immigrant fresh from Ellis Island, who lived in a tiny closet off the kitchen and helped with the housework. Yes, money was a positive good. There was no muckraking of Rockefeller or Ford at 65 Fort Washington Avenue.

The most obvious sign of prosperity was a car. Our first Model A Ford was soon upgraded to a Buick with folding jump seats and a vase of artificial flowers in the back. The car was used for summer vacations along the New Jersey shore. The choice of a vacation spot was not accidental. Eastern European Jews who arrived in the United States in recent decades had discovered the Catskills, north of the city. Well-to-do German Jews had established a summer colony on the Jersey coast as far back as the 1880s, when it was known as the "Jewish Newport." The bungalows we rented in Bradley Beach or Deal bore no resemblance to their Victorian mansions overlooking the ocean, but we had backyards where Edgar and I could pull our little sisters in a wagon and pump a rickety swing. Most of our time was spent at the beach hopping in and out of the waves, building sand castles, and collecting shells. By the summer's end, my face was covered with freckles and my hair curlier than ever.

Our car spent winters on blocks in a garage, but in fall and spring it was used for trips to Philadelphia to see Mother's family, who were also Jews of German descent. Grandpa Levi Darmstadter was a balding little man who complained of the cost (rising) of the meat on the table and the behavior of the *Schwartze* who ate too much on her weekly cleaning day. Grandmother Mary was nervous and frail; my one fond memory of her is that she bundled up the comic pages of the *Philadelphia Sunday Inquirer* and mailed them to us. Since the *New York Times* carried no comics I would never have known about the Katzenjammer Kids and Hairbreadth Harry if it had not been for Grandma Mary.

Mother's younger brother, Herbert, was a doctor with his office in the front room of their house on Old York Road. When we visited, all the Philadelphia family came to see us. There was a steady procession from Uncle Herbert's office, where he thumped chests and took blood pressures, to the dining room where

Dad dispensed legal advice. Grandpa's sisters, Aunts Miriam and Henrietta, maiden women in their sixties, were the only affluent members of the Darmstadter family. Aunt Miriam made an excellent living as a dressmaker, sewing fine clothes for Philadelphia's Main Line, and Aunt Henrietta was a buyer for Snellenburg's Department Store who made annual buying trips to Europe. A bosomy woman in a tailored suit and no-nonsense shoes, she resembled her contemporary, Gertrude Stein. Although she was the only woman I had ever met who held down a man's job and could discuss politics and investments with Dad, I did not like her because she was an Old Maid. I had learned from a card game played with Grandma Celia that Old Maids were skinny, plain, unloved—the worst fate that could befall a girl. Never mind that Aunt Henrietta and Aunt Miriam lived comfortably and sent postcards every summer showing themselves in front of the Eiffel Tower or feeding the pigeons at St. Mark's. Or that Henrietta's sharp intelligence was apparent when she discussed current affairs with Dad. She had no husband; therefore she was to be looked down on as an Old Maid and shunned lest her defect be catching.

The year the war ended I bade a cheerful farewell to Mrs. Lapham and entered public school. P.S. 46, at the corner of 156th Street and St. Nicholas Avenue, had been built during the Civil War as a hospital for convalescent soldiers. Although remodeled since its glory days, it was a forbidding structure with narrow windows and scarred wooden desks bolted to the floor. Probably because New York's schools were overcrowded, educators had developed a system called Rapid Advance for any pupil who showed ability. I advanced rapidly, covering first grade in a semester, then second, then third. By the time I was nine—and small for my age—I was in sixth grade. Those school years remain a blur. My classmates were all bigger, tougher, and more worldly wise than I. Although I learned arithmetic and geography, I never caught on to the popular mores, the songs and slang that were in vogue.

During this time my family became Christian Scientists. If I mention this today people nod wisely and say, "Of course. They were trying to escape being Jewish." In the 1920s a considerable number of Jews joined the Christian Science Church and the Ethical Culture Society; some also shortened their names and noses in an attempt at passing. But for us the impetus to change came from Mother's relations with her friend Bella Fishman. Despite Mother's brains and efficiency, she lacked self-confidence and was easily swayed by what "they" said and did. Aunt Bella—a courtesy title—was a large, positive woman whose charming manner concealed a will of iron. The dominant figure in Mother's small circle, she advised her on how to furnish her home and bring up her children.

When she and her husband, Uncle Abe, who was a head shorter than his wife, became Christian Scientists, Mother and Dad followed.

Alice's and my knowledge of the new religion came on Thursdays, after Wednesday night testimonial meetings. Then we would hear tales of remarkable conversions and cures, often brought about by pure-minded children. One story concerned a little girl— "no older than you"—who interrupted a burglar at work. She appealed to his better nature by telling him that God was Love and he left the apartment empty-handed. The Rover boys could have done no better. The drama of Wednesday nights was not equaled in Sunday School, where we were taught Bible stories and hymns. When I visited Grandma Celia I proudly sang for her, in my usual off-key:

> "Onward, Christian soldiers
> Marching as to war
> With the cross of Jesus
> Going on before."

I was halfway through the stanza when I saw tears in Grandma's eyes. Christmas trees, all right, but she never expected to encounter "the cross of Jesus" in her living room. Although she was too mild-mannered to expostulate, I never sang hymns for her again.

Grandma did not have to suffer her family's apostasy for long, because there was a schism in the

Christian Science Church, and the Fishmans left the Mother Church with my parents docilely following. For several years Alice and I went to the Fishmans' apartment on Sundays, where Uncle Abe instructed the older children and Aunt Bella the younger ones. All I can remember of these Sundays is a paper I wrote titled "There is Nothing Either Good nor Bad but Thinking Makes It So." Uncle Abe and I were sure that the sentiment came from Jesus; much later I found that the phrase was Hamlet's (Act 2, Scene 2).

Aunt Bella's influence on Mother continued. The summer that I was eight, she proposed that my parents forsake the Jersey shore and go instead to Milford, Connecticut, on Long Island Sound, where they could share a small bungalow that would seem roomier if their older children went to camp. Camp Newfound, a Christian Science camp in Harrison, Maine, was built on a narrow, sandy peninsula jutting out into a lake. When the rains came, days and days of downpour, the peninsula was under water, and we traveled from bunk to mess hall balancing precariously on wooden planks. True to the "See no evil, speak no evil" tradition of Christian Science, we were forbidden to discuss the weather or the plague of mosquitoes that accompanied it. As the youngest child in camp there were few sched-uled activities for me except swimming. I spent most of my days in the woods, where the rains had encouraged a lush growth of mosses, ferns, and brightly colored mushrooms. Stretched out on the soft green moss with a book, I was not actively unhappy, although I understood in some dim recess of my mind that I had been sent to camp in order to make life easier for my mother. Yet I never spoke of my dissatisfaction or protested when I was enrolled in Newfound for a second summer. Perhaps one reason that I kept silent was a sudden improvement in my school situation.

Mother had read that some Teachers College psychologists were organizing an experimental class for "gifted" children. She wrote, setting forth my qualifications, and soon afterward a woman appeared at my classroom door to ask that I be excused for an hour. Miss Margaret V. Cobb, thin and acne-scarred, resembled the Old Maid card in Grandma's game rather than the succoring angel she turned out to be. In a small office next to the principal's, she gave me my first intelligence test. Within weeks my parents received a letter from Dr. Leta S. Hollingworth of Teachers College inviting me to join the Special Opportunity Class. Before Christmas 1922, I began riding a double-decker bus down Broadway each morning to P.S. 165 at 109th Street, where I joined a group of girls and boys who had been misfits or loners in their schools. Many were younger and smaller than I—and some were brighter.

Dr. Hollingworth, who had a grant from the Carnegie Corporation for a three-year study of "gifted" children in New York's public schools, was a pleasant-looking woman of thirty-five, her brown hair worn in a braid around her head, her clothes tailored with scant attention to fashion. Educated in Nebraska, she had completed her Ph.D. at Columbia University, where her senior professor, Edward L. Thorndike, still declared it wasteful to give women higher education because they were innately mediocre. She established, through a series of carefully crafted studies, that women's intellectual capacity equaled men's and that, contrary to the then current belief, women were not periodically incapacitated by menstruation. Her pioneering work won her membership in New York's Heterodoxy Club, a group of radical feminists whose ranks included Fannie Hurst, Mable Dodge Luhan, Mary Heaton Vorse, and Elizabeth Gurley Flynn.

I knew none of this at the time or even a decade later when, as a college student, I lunched with Dr. Hollingworth at her apartment on Morningside Heights. Soft-spoken and reticent, she gave no hint of the part she had played in establishing women's claim to equality. Her untimely death in 1939 deprived me of further opportunity to learn her history. It is only through recent biographies of her and her contemporaries that I realize how fortunate I was to have been one of her guinea pigs in what proved to be my most significant educational experience.

Close to My Heart

The Special Opportunity Class—which we always called Spec Op—was designed to study the physical and psychological characteristics of bright children as well as experiment with teaching methods and curricula that would benefit them. Of the fifty-odd children in the class, whose IQs ranged from 135 to 190, all but three or four were Jewish. To a considerable extent this reflected the predominately Jewish population in the city's public schools in the 1920s. But it also illustrated the blind side of mental testing which, then as now, failed to take socioeconomic factors into account. Even Dr. Hollingworth had written in an early book: "Paupers are very stupid as a group. A lengthy bibliography of scientific studies exists to establish this fact beyond a doubt."

The selection of children for Spec Op, supposedly based on a citywide search, was not conducted scientifically. Rather we were chosen when a teacher or parent brought our talents to Dr. Hollingworth's attention. Teachers College was less than a mile from Harlem, but Miss Cobb was never dispatched to the east side of Morningside Park to test African-American children; nor did she go to Chinatown. Thus we were led to believe that bright children were largely from Jewish immigrant backgrounds, while our few Irish and Scottish classmates added diversity. We never encountered African-Americans, Asians,

Italians, or the other national groups in our polyglot city.

Our classroom was the largest, brightest room in the school, with cabinets under the windows that housed an encyclopedia, dictionary, microscope, and mimeograph machine, equipment unheard of in public schools. Our teacher, Miss Sheeky, took us through the standard curriculum, but there was little learning by rote. We were exhilarated by the exchange of ideas and could scarcely wait to report our findings. Instead of the bolted-down desks of P.S. 46, Spec Op's were lightweight and movable. As hands waved wildly, begging to be called on, desks inched forward until at the end of a morning Miss Sheeky was barricaded and we had to scoot backward to allow her to leave.

In addition to learning the three R's, we were taken on trips to the American Museum of Natural History, the Metropolitan Museum of Art, and to factories and city markets. M. Henry Olinger came from Columbia twice a week to teach us French, and Dr. Hollingworth herself introduced us to Biography. We researched the lives of eminent people, writing biographies to be read to the class. A catchy opening was more important than a birthdate if we wanted to win the interest of our hearers, so we selected anecdotes rather than merely listing accomplishments. Among the subjects I "biographized"—the class's word—were George Eliot, Mark Twain, and yes, Mary Baker Eddy, the founder of Christian Science. Biography not only shaped my reading habits but influenced my choice of subjects when, almost three decades later, I began to write books for children.

And then there were the intelligence tests, weekly, monthly. Sometimes it seemed as if every psychologist in the country had devised a new test to be tried out on us. If the results conformed to those Miss Cobb had found, well and good; if not, it was back to the drawing board. Our parents were tested, our sisters and brothers, even our grandparents. We not only knew our own IQs but those of everyone else in the class. Were we conceited by hearing that we were "gifted"? Not at all, because there was Donald, with a genius rating of 190, and Herman, with an IQ of 180, who chose to "biographize" Mohammed and spent his free hours reading the dictionary, from AARDVARK to ZULU. Miss Cobb informed me that I was at the class median, with an IQ of 165. When I came in second in classroom tests she repeatedly marveled that I was performing better than expected. She need not have been surprised. Mother went over my homework every night, drilling me. If I scored a B rather than an A, she came to school to find out what was wrong. Dad called her "one hundred percent Elsie."

Except for Donald and Herman, we were normal girls and boys, enjoying school after years of boredom and loneliness. We played chess and checkers, and worked crossword puzzles, which were just becoming popular. The boys were avid baseball fans. Some of the girls were interested in clothes and movie stars and one could do the Charleston. Except that all of us talked at once, eager to have a say, there were no behavior problems. Nor were there any precocious romances, none of the conventional "Tom loves Susy," "Sadie loves John," and little whispering about sex. We were children, excited by our studies and by the opportunity to make friends for the first time.

While I was in Spec Op my father dreamed that I became a writer—famous of course. Now when people asked, "What are you going to do when you grow up?" I answered, "Write books." So, I note from a tattered Spec Op memory book, did four other girls in the class. None of us planned to be housewives and mothers. The boys' aspirations were more varied. In the same book I find that they wanted to be lawyers, scientists, doctors, movie producers, even a leader of Tammany Hall.

Spec Op had not obliterated gender differences, as we learned in our last year when the boys left the room for a special science class while the girls remained behind for sewing. Indignant, I drew up a petition that all the girls signed asking that we too be permitted to study science. Miss Sheeky was so angry at our temerity that she refused to speak to us until our mothers came to school to apologize. Where was Dr.

Hollingworth? I can only speculate that she could go so far and no further with the public school bureaucracy. For the balance of the term we sewed slips to wear to graduation.

My chagrin at missing science led to my first venture into feminist politics. Class officers were elected twice a year. Because boys were in the majority, they always won the major offices, with a token girl as vice-president or secretary. But as I pointed out in the privacy of sewing class, if we selected an all-girl slate instead of scattering our votes, we could win. For the last semester of Spec Op the class had a female president, vice-president, secretary, and treasurer.

Politics was in the air in 1924. Someone brought a radio to class so we could listen to the campaign speeches. President Warren G. Harding had died the summer before, leaving behind a record of scandal and corruption. Most of the class were Democrats. We thought we were rooting for the underdog when we opposed Republican Calvin Coolidge and backed John W. Davis instead. I still have the BACK TO HONESTY WITH DAVIS button that I wore on my jacket that fall. Fortunately, I was unable to look ahead to 1954, when the Supreme Court heard the case of Brown vs. the Board of Education and John W. Davis was the lawyer for the southern segregationists.

Radio had come into my life a few years earlier when a friend of Edgar's had given us a homemade crystal set. With headphones and patience one might hear a broadcast from KDKA in Pittsburgh, the pioneer radio station. Later we acquired a store-bought set, but there was little interesting about radio then except its novelty. I was well into adolescence before news and entertainment programs were specially written for the medium. Which made ours the last generation to depend on the printed word for amusement and enlightenment.

Except for the movies. On Saturdays we saw Douglas Fairbanks in *The Three Musketeers*, Mary Pickford in *Daddy Long Legs*, Charlie Chaplin's *The Gold Rush*, and Lon Chaney in *The Hunchback of Notre Dame*, unaware that decades later these films would be shown at the Museum of Modern Art as classics of the silent screen. Going to the movies took stamina. The program started with a newsreel followed by cartoons, two-reelers starring Harold Lloyd or Our Gang, and a serial that ended with the heroine in a burning building and the subtitle "Continued Next Week." Only then came the feature film. As the theater lights dimmed and the piano player struck his first chord, we suspended belief, ready to laugh at the comics, cheer the good guys, and hiss the villains. I doubt that our moral values were impaired by the fact that virtue always triumphed and the villains were punished. But the stereotypes of people of other races made an impression. Farina with the rolling eyes, the butt of jokes in

Our Gang comedies, handkerchief-headed Aunt Jemima, and shuffling Stepin Fetchit assured audiences that black people were inferior. And as the Hearst newspapers warned of "the Yellow Peril" and Congress passed an immigration act virtually excluding Asians, the serials specialized in featuring Chinese villains. For years I had dreams of white slave traders and smoky opium dens.

Spec Op graduation was a grand affair attended by our Teachers College sponsors and members of the Board of Education. I opened the program with the salutatory address, a pedestrian speech written by my mother, and Herman closed with the valedictory. Instead of expressing sadness at leaving friends or concern for a better world, his topic was "Mankind's goal — success. By success only may joy be obtained." Why would I find this surprising? The year was 1925, the second year of Coolidge's presidency, when a man with a mission, as Mark Sullivan wrote in *Our Times*, was "a man with a mission to sell more automobiles, more chewing gum, more shaving soap."

CHAPTER

2

Shortly after I entered Spec Op, our family moved downtown, to 157 West 79th Street, between Amsterdam and Columbus Avenues. The move from a Washington Heights walkup to an elevator apartment building on the Upper West Side was a significant step up the ladder. Everything in the new apartment was bigger and brighter. There was a piano in the living room foretelling music lessons, and Alice's and my room was furnished with Early American maple pieces and blue candlewick bedspreads. Even the maid, no longer a green girl, had a reasonably sized room and a bathroom with a tub. It sometimes struck me as curious that she had a bathroom to herself while the four of us shared one that was not much larger, but I did not understand the class bias of apartment house builders in those years.

I traveled to Spec Op by subway, dropping a nickel in the turnstile at the 79th Street station and getting off at 110th Street. After school I went to the Museum of Natural History, only two blocks away, or to Central Park, bird book in hand. No one was concerned then about sex and the city child. Mother had done her literal best to instruct me in the facts of life, reading aloud from a pamphlet about the birds and the bees that she had obtained from the U.S. Children's Bureau. Although I could tell from her grave voice that this was important, I could not fathom what it had to do with me. Nor was I much clearer a couple of years later when she prepared me for menstruation, which she called "falling off the roof" or "the curse." She explained that it all had to do with future babies; no mention was made of the role of the opposite sex.

Aware that some big secret was being kept from us, my friends and I pooled our information, to little avail. What were we to make of the flashers—the seedy looking men on Riverside Drive who walked toward us with their flies open while we giggled and averted our eyes? Or the feelers we encountered in the movies? More times than I can count, when we went to Loews 83rd Street Theatre on Saturday afternoons, a man would seat himself beside us and begin to stroke our skirts or legs. Seasoned city children, we promptly moved to another part of the theater. Had he followed us, we would have told an usher, but he never did. And we certainly did not tell our parents, for fear that our movie excursions might be forbidden.

Ignorance reigned until a young man sat on the grass next to me in Central Park one afternoon. Sketch pad in hand, he proceeded to draw the male and female sex organs and explain coitus. I listened, fascinated. The drawings were clear and his explanation well phrased. It was not until he suggested that we withdraw into the bushes so that he could demonstrate the procedure that I thanked him politely and walked away. He too did not follow me. Why were sex offenders so much less offensive in the 1920s? At the dinner table that night I reported the incident to my parents. From the glances they exchanged I could tell that something important had happened. But although they solemnly warned me not to speak to strange men, they offered no explanations and did not forbid me to go to the park.

I could hardly wait to get to school the next day to pass along the information I had acquired. Undoubtedly it was true—the expressions on my parents' faces confirmed it—but it was hard to believe. Our parents, our *grandparents*, did *that*? Surely there was some missing ingredient that we did not know.

Shortly after moving downtown my family abandoned Christian Science. I had precipitated the break. When I had a wretched cold, a sneezy, wheezy affair, Mother took me to the office of a Christian Science practitioner a few blocks away. The practitioner looked at my streaming eyes and nose, then asked sternly, "What bad thoughts have you been holding?" I was so indignant at her lack of sympathy that I got up and walked out of her office. My parents must have been ready because the next time I had a cold I received coddling and chicken soup.

The break with Christian Science meant finis to Camp Newfound. For five summers, from 1924 to 1928, I went to Camp Fernwood, in Poland, Maine. Set in a forest of pine and fir, Fernwood had well-tended playing fields and a path through the woods to the lake where there were docks and a fleet of canoes. Unlike Newfound, everything at Fernwood was ship-shape. Ten bunkhouses, each housing ten campers and a counselor, were as neat as army barracks. I learned to make a bed with hospital corners and use a broom before daily inspection. I swam three times a day, earning a Junior Lifesaving emblem, which entitled me to paddle a canoe. I rode horseback, went on overnight hikes and canoe trips, and, in my final camp summer, climbed Mount Washington, the highest peak in the White Mountains. Although I was poor in baseball, inept in basketball, and hopeless in track, my athletic failures were compensated for by my joy in nature study. The athletic counselors were young Amazons eagerly pursued by lovesick campers. No one had a crush on the nature counselor, a shy, plain-looking biology student. But I spent every free hour with her, absorbing all she could tell me about the trees, flowers, and birds, and the lore that went with them.

Like most adolescents, we were awash in sentimentality. We had crushes on counselors; we had best friends. We gloried in being part of a group—bunkmates, teammates—and our emotions were enhanced by moonlit evenings around the campfire, when even monotones like me joined in the singing. At summer's end, when, for the last time, we sang (to the tune of "We Gather Together to Ask the Lord's Blessing"), "We hail thee our camp / And sing your praises / Our hearts will be loyal / For the rest of our days," I blinked away a tear just as the others did.

The sense of belonging that I found at Camp Fernwood did not carry over to high school. When Spec Op ended, our Teachers College mentors suggested two alternatives: George Washington High School, a big new public school in the Bronx, or Dalton High School, a private school on West 73rd Street, which offered partial scholarships to Spec Op graduates. My parents chose Dalton, only a six-block walk from home, with a snob appeal that George Washington lacked.

Dalton in 1925 was considerably more experimental than Spec Op had been. The Dalton Plan (the name came from Dalton, Massachusetts, where it was first introduced) was devised by Helen Parkhurst in the belief that students must be permitted to absorb knowledge at their own pace. She had started Children's University—"Kids U," pupils irreverently called it—in 1919, attracting parents interested in progressive education. Dalton High School, opening several years later, had not yet sent graduates to college. By importing youngsters from Spec Op, Miss Parkhurst doubtless hoped to have students who would continue their education and thus give the school academic standing.

When I entered Dalton, the plan called for monthly assignments in each subject—chapters to read, problems to solve, poems to memorize—which we could complete in any sequence we chose. Desks and bells were nonexistent. We could spend two hours reading at a table in the English room, then tackle History, leaving Latin and Math to the end. Many did this.

The plan may have worked in elementary school, where Alice was enrolled, but problems arose in high school, because college-bound students were required to cover specific subject matter for College Board exams. Consequently, the program was constantly being tinkered with, until much of our day was spent in conventional classes. Because the school was housed in a barely remodeled one-family residence, there was no place for a science laboratory. Girls were not expected to study science anyway, but mathematics was a College Board requirement. After three years of trying to find a teacher who would kindle enthusiasm for math, the administration imported a veritable dragon who drilled us relentlessly in algebra and geometry.

Close to My Heart

I do not recall any art or music save for interpretive dancing taught by Anita Zahn, a follower of Isadora Duncan's. Barefooted, wearing Grecian-style chiffon tunics, we lumbered across the room swirling scarves to express ourselves to the music of Victrola records. A chubby adolescent with little sense of rhythm, I could only express agony. Watching me, Miss Zahn doubtless felt the same way.

Many of my classmates were the daughters and granddaughters of department store founders, with names like Saks, Gimbel, and Namm. Unwelcome at the city's posh finishing schools because they were Jewish, they looked on Dalton as a place to mark time until they married. Coming to school in chauffeured limousines, often accompanied by a governess, they wore Chanel blouses with pearls, the fashion trademark of the late 1920s, while I walked to school in a middy blouse and pleated skirt. Treating me as a kid sister, they talked freely to me at lunch. Thus I learned about their visits to speakeasies and their weekend dances. Judy, the prettiest girl in the class, was absent for a few days, blinded temporarily by bootleg gin. Sixteen-year-old Marie was absent, too, after an abortion — and the father of the fetus was a department store scion. By senior year, two or three of the girls made Saturday lunch dates with me, but I was never invited to their parties, nor did I expect to be.

The only time I rode in a classmate's limousine was at Thanksgiving in 1928, when a school administrator, probably Miss Parkhurst, decided that it would be educational for us to give Thanksgiving dinners to the poor. The school arranged everything, buying turkeys and fixings and procuring names of worthy families. I rode to the Lower East Side in Joyce's car. When we reached the address we had been given, the chauffeur, clearly disapproving, grabbed the laden basket and led us up the narrow tenement stairs. Overwhelmed by the dark room, the smells of cooking, and the stammered thanks of the recipient, we fled down the stairs and rode uptown in silence. I'm not sure what this lesson was supposed to teach, but it certainly taught me that Lady Bountiful was not a role that I cared to play.

Although I had begun to suspect that I was a maverick, I was not unhappy at Dalton. I liked what remained of the plan's freedom of choice, the hours I could spend reading after my assignments were done. Doubtless because of my highly motivated mother, the plan seemed to work for me. In my senior year I won a $5 gold piece for an essay on "School Spirit" and was chosen valedictorian. My address at commencement in May 1929 praised the training in self-reliance that we had received, which had taught us to think rather than parrot back our teachers' beliefs. This would, I predicted, help us to handle our new freedom in college and afterward. Perhaps so, but more lessons in science and math would not have been amiss either.

While in high school I learned more about the hierarchy among Jews. Walking along Central Park West with my father, he paused in front of Temple Sherith Israel on 70th Street to say, "*They* are better than we are." "They" were the Spanish and Portuguese Jews who had come to America in the seventeenth and eighteenth centuries. With names like Cardoza, Baruch, and Seixas, they had become merchants and bankers before the German Jewish migration. The German Jews, too, had their pecking order. The earlier arrivals who became bankers and railroad magnates looked down on latecomers who founded department stores and hence were "in trade." Both groups lived on the East Side in New York, spent summers in New Jersey, and winter vacations in Palm Beach—never Miami. If they were affiliated with a temple, it was Temple Emanu-El, the "cathedral" of Reform Judaism. Blackballed by New York's Racquet and University clubs, they belonged to the Harmonie Club and, after golf became fashionable, to the Century Country Club in Purchase, N.Y.

That still left us, the German Jews who had not made it big—not yet, anyway. When a classmate invited Alice to the Harmonie Club, my parents were delighted, although Dad pointed out, "*They* wouldn't let me join." Nor would "they" accept him in the

Century Club when he took up golf. Instead he joined the Broadmoor Club on the new Hutchinson River Parkway. Broadmoor admitted German Jews but blackballed those whose parents came from Eastern Europe.

No matter how divided they were among themselves, Spanish, Portuguese and German Jews agreed that *they* were superior to the two million Jews from eastern Europe who poured into the United States between 1880 and 1920 and who vastly outnumbered the early-comers. Fleeing pogroms and Czarist oppression, these Jews were "foreign," "oriental." They spoke Yiddish, wore prayer shawls and yarmulkes, ate kosher food, and celebrated the Sabbath on Saturdays. They were also perceived as having hooked noses, loud voices, and singsong accents. Fearful that the arrival of these ignorant strangers would increase anti-Semitism, the German Jews hastened to differentiate themselves from the newcomers. Because so many Russian names ended in "ki" or "ky," the assimilated Jews called them "kikes," thus adding a new pejorative to the American vocabulary of racism.

By the 1920s, numbers of Eastern European Jews had escaped the Lower East Side ghetto. There were Yiddish-speaking millionaires on Park Avenue, and a prosperous middle class was finding its way to "our" neighborhood. To distinguish themselves from these newcomers, Mother used to say, so often that it became a family joke, "Don't know a word of Yiddish" and "Never had herring in the house." We also never had bagels or lox, not even the expensive kind called Nova Scotia salmon. Dad made fun of my music teacher, who had a prominent nose and pronounced "singing" with a hard "g," and laughed about a family who had changed its name from Washinsky to Wall when renting an apartment on Park Avenue. To remind them of their origins, some joker had subscribed to the *Jewish Daily Forward* in their name; the Yiddish-language newspaper was left on their doormat each morning.

More than a half-century after the Holocaust, it is hard to believe these distinctions, but they were real then. One childhood friend whose family *did* belong to the Harmonie Club remembers that when her mother planned a Sweet Sixteen party for her she crossed off her guest list all those who were "kikes." Another recalls her mother saying, "I'd rather have you marry a *goy* than a kike." My parents tactfully said, "She's not our kind" when I brought home an acquaintance of doubtful ancestry.

Puzzling over these distinctions, I began to wonder what Judaism was all about. Shortly before my fourteenth birthday I astonished my parents by saying that I wanted to go to Jewish Sunday School and be confirmed. Confirmation was the Reform Jewish coming-of-age ceremony, corresponding to the bar mitzvah, which was only for boys. Although Dad, characteristically, said I only wanted confirmation presents, he enrolled me in Sunday School, choosing Temple Emanu-El, of course.

In the year that I attended, the congregation was building its magnificent new temple at 65th Street and Fifth Avenue and in the interim was sharing quarters with Temple Beth-El some blocks to the north. Every Sunday morning a team of rabbis lectured the confirmation class on Jewish history and religion. The teaching was perfunctory, the discipline poor, and the atmosphere decidedly secular. We spent more time whispering, passing around candy, and giggling at the boys than in serious discussion. Any hope I had had for a spiritual experience was further dashed when, in the weeks before confirmation, we were given typed copies of the speeches we were to make at the ceremony. A rabbi had written all of the speeches. I was insulted, not only by his turgid prose (Mother could have done better) but also by the fact that we could not be trusted to speak for ourselves at what was supposed to be a turning point in our lives. I considered dropping out then, but a classmate urged me to remain, insisting that the ceremony itself and the rabbi's blessing would be inspiring.

The ceremony, in May 1928, was endless as more than sixty girls and boys spoke on "Piety toward God" (my topic), "Sin and Repentance," "Immortality," and "Devotion to Parents," parroting the words that the rabbi had written. I joined in the confirmation hymn, recited the Twenty-third Psalm, then awaited the rabbi's blessing. But there was to be no epiphany for me. As he moved along the row of confirmants, I scarcely heard what he was saying, so conscious was I of the drops of his saliva falling onto our bowed heads.

Feeling as if I had given religion a fair chance, I announced at the dinner table a few days later, "I don't believe in God." "But you must believe in something," Mother protested. "Why?" Dad and I asked simultaneously. End of discussion.

It is tempting to say that Temple Emanu-El's confirmation class had made me a confirmed atheist. But there were other influences as well. The years in Christian Science had provided a good breeding ground for skepticism. Besides, I was reading Sinclair Lewis and H. L. Mencken, debunkers of religion as well as other aspects of the American scene. Confirmed atheist I might have been, but I was not a confirmed cynic, for I kept a photograph of Charles A. Lindbergh on my bureau after he made his solo flight across the Atlantic and knew the words to "Lucky Lindy," that year's pop song. My other hero then was Governor Al Smith, who I thought represented the common people in the 1928 presidential election. When Herbert Hoover defeated him, I wept.

My enthusiasm for Al Smith, later a spokesman for big business, was part of my general confusion about values. For while I relished the Mencken-Lewis scorn for the get-rich atmosphere of the day, what was wrong with making money? All of my parents' friends were doing it. And not old-fashioned money earned by the sweat of their brows, but funny money from the stock market.

I can scarcely remember a time when I did not know about the bulls and bears of the stock exchange. Even the staid *New York Times* ran front-page stories when Radio (Radio Corporation of America) went up 18 points in a single day, or General Motors passed the 150 mark. Uncle Manny spent most of his day in his broker's office watching the ticker tape. His stock market gains had enabled him to move to a larger apartment and to employ two maids and a chauffeur. To celebrate their twentieth wedding anniversary, he and Aunt Alma gave a party at the Ritz, where I had my first taste of caviar. Dad, whose law office was now on 43rd Street, in the same building as the *New Yorker*, was investing (no one then would have called it speculating) all of his spare cash in the market. On margin, of course, so that he would make a lot of money if the upward spiral continued — or lose everything. Encouraged by the Hoover bull market, our family moved down the street to 118 West 79th Street, which had a doorman and two elevators, one for tenants, the other for servants and delivery boys. Our current maid was an accomplished cook; a laundress came from Harlem to do the wash, and when Mother gave dinner parties, a waitress arrived hours beforehand to set the table with a sumptuous cloth and to mold butter into the shape of roses and leaves.

Menus were more sophisticated, too, as Mother and her friends became Jewish housewives with catholic tastes. They now served oysters, shrimp, and lobster, dishes their parents would have refused to eat. Broccoli, unheard of on Washington Heights, had become a fashionable vegetable, in large part because of a *New Yorker* cartoon, often reprinted, in which a child, urged to eat broccoli, says, "I say it's spinach, and I say the hell with it." Salads made an appearance, too—wedges of iceberg lettuce with Russian dressing.

Neither my grandparents or parents were drinkers, but after a decade of Prohibition solid bourgeois folk began breaking the law. Dad bought whiskey from a bootlegger and at least once made bathtub gin, which was prepared in the kitchen with alcohol (purchased with a doctor's prescription) and juniper berries. Since gin was the easiest drink to make in a New York apartment, the first drinks my generation tasted were Orange Blossoms—gin and orange juice—or Bronx cocktails, which added vermouth to the mixture. No one was concerned about breaking the law. In 1929 it was a greater crime to pass a red light when driving than to drink a cocktail.

Mother adjusted to the changing times by bobbing her hair and wearing tailored shirtmaker dresses, transforming herself from plump hausfrau to trim matron. On special occasions when she and Dad went to the theater or to the opening of the Roxy, a splashy motion picture palace on 49th Street, she wore an evening dress while Dad sported a tuxedo and top hat. She tried to pass along her new sense of style to me, but it was not easy. For one thing, I lacked the flat-chested boyish figure—the flapper depicted in John Held, Jr. cartoons—that was then in vogue. Even after I lost my childhood chubbiness, brassieres and girdles could not conceal my natural curves. And there was still my untamable hair, which could never be made to resemble the fashionable shingle or boyish bob.

I used lipstick and rouge and plucked my barely visible blonde eyebrows. But the first time I used mascara I was caught in the rain and returned home with black streaks on my cheeks. Mother was so new to makeup herself that she could not advise me, although she did her best to see that I was well dressed. During the years of our new prosperity, she bought me a nutria coat (not quite beaver, but almost) and a red fox fur piece with beady eyes and a jaw firmly clamped to its tail. Since several of my parents' friends were clothing manufacturers, we bought our dresses wholesale, going to 7th Avenue showrooms on Saturday mornings. Our shoes came from Saks Fifth Avenue and our hats from Salingers, a milliner who was beginning to make a name for herself. When I was dressed up, my pocketbook matched my shoes, my gloves matched my pocketbook, and my skirt was the height that was in fashion that year. But even though I followed the rules, I did not feel smartly turned out. I could not understand how my contemporaries knew what "they" were wearing. Who were those arbiters of fashion and how did one learn to anticipate their dictates? I never discovered this, not in 1929 and not today.

If I had problems with my clothes, I had even more with boys, who were appearing on the horizon in a new guise. Younger than most of my friends, I thought of boys as I had in Spec Op, companions to play with and even compete against. On the rare occasion when a boy asked me to the movies or escorted me to a party, I invariably broke some unwritten law. Often it started at the beginning of the evening when the elevator reached the main floor and my escort dropped back to permit me to leave first. I strode ahead purposefully. When I reached the heavy vestibule door I pulled it open. "You shouldn't do that," he would scold. "I'm supposed to open the door." If he had borrowed his father's car, I made the same mistake, opening the car door and seating myself without assistance. Nor did I ever get the hang of switching places as we walked down the street. Was he supposed to walk on the outside to protect me from a runaway horse, or on the inside to receive the contents of a carelessly aimed slop bucket? And how did one maneuver when changing directions at a street corner? "All you have to do," a popular friend advised, "is to look up at him and say, 'I think you're wonderful.'" But I could not do that, so boys rarely called a second time.

That's when Mother began sighing. She didn't sigh much between Monday and Friday, but she sighed loudly and often if I didn't have a date on Saturday. Staying home alone on Saturdays was, if not shameful, at least something that one did not discuss, like bad breath. It was hard at first to convince me of this, because I liked being home alone. It gave me a chance to read the books on Mother's bed table, books like Vina Delmar's *Bad Girl* which she had expressly warned me against. In the long run Mother's sighs, like a trickle of water on a rock, had some effect. Even Alice, who was more popular than I, but never popular enough to satisfy Mother, heeded them. She was in her seventies and happily married for a half-century when she confided that if she and her husband had no date for Saturday night she felt unwanted. Sometimes I have the same feeling.

CHAPTER

3

My high school graduation present in 1929 was a trip across the United States with a chaperone and a group of girls. Edgar went to Europe that fateful summer. While I was out West, Wellesley College accepted me as a freshman. Because I was tired of being younger than my classmates I proposed that I stay out of school for a year; to my surprise, Mother and Dad agreed. I planned "to loaf and invite my soul" — I had been reading Whitman — but Mother got me a job at Dalton. The school had moved to a new building on East 89th Street with every modern facility, including a swimming pool, which I was permitted to use. I worked in the mimeograph office and tended the telephone switchboard when the regular operator was at lunch. It was a complicated board with a tangle of spaghetti-like wires, and I had a hard time getting the hang of it. One dark day I cut off Miss Parkhurst's calls, not once but twice. I was immediately fired.

I had not deliberately sabotaged my parents' effort to keep me busy, but for someone who did not want a job, my timing was excellent. The week I left Dalton, the stock market went down, down, down. While President Hoover declared that "the fundamental business of the country" was basically sound, stock prices continued to fall. By November, millions were unemployed. My father lost his lifetime's savings. Uncle Manny and Aunt Alma dismissed their maids and chauffeur and moved to a smaller apartment; Edgar—by then known as Eddie—dropped out of college in the hope of assisting his family. Fortunately, Dad's law practice remained intact, although it was harder to collect fees.

With Mother still objecting to my "lying around the house all day reading," I left the apartment with Dad every morning. Usually I went to the 42nd Street library. Sometimes I sat in the main reading room investigating the reference works that lined the walls. On other days I checked out an armload of books and crossed the street to Stern's department store, where the ladies room offered comfortable chairs. I read rapidly and omnivorously—novels, biographies, plays—as uncritically as a television addict might watch her screen today.

At times I varied this routine to meet Eddie, who was also at loose ends. Often we spent the day at the Metropolitan Museum of Art, making our way from the Egyptian rooms to the paintings upstairs. In the good old days a month or two earlier, Uncle Manny had been a museum patron, so that when we tired of walking we could attend the lectures open to members' families.

Saturdays I had a different program. I had begun to read "The Conning Tower," a column in *The World* edited by FPA (Franklin Pierce Adams) that included light verse, puns, and anecdotes from George S. Kaufman, Dorothy Parker, Robert Benchley, and Heywood Broun (whose column "It Seems to Me" also appeared in *The World*). This group of writers frequently met for lunch at the Algonquin Hotel, on 43rd Street, where a large round table was set aside for their use. Accompanied by a friend, I too had lunch at the Algonquin. Perhaps in those post-crash months business was slow, because the head waiter seated us near the round table, where we could see and often overhear their conversation. From a recent biography of Dorothy Parker I have learned that she and her table mates were aware of sightseers like us and would raise their voices and shape their ripostes for our benefit.

We did not linger over coffee but hurried to Leblang's or Gray's drug store for cut-rate tickets to a matinee. With my parents' Theatre Guild subscription, which introduced me to George Bernard Shaw and Eugene O'Neill and the bargain matinees on Saturdays, I saw everything significant or amusing that Broadway had to offer: *Front Page*, by Ben Hecht and Charles MacArthur, *June Moon*, by Ring Lardner and George S. Kaufman, Marc Connolly's *Green Pastures*, and so on.

Mother's Saturday night sighs had diminished after I met a boy (we were "girls" and "boys" even in our twenties) who didn't care, didn't even notice if I opened the vestibule door myself. David admired "The Conning Tower" although he would never rubberneck at the Algonquin. He laughed at Marx Brothers movies and at Stoopnagle and Budd, popular radio comics, but basically he was an intellectual, the first I'd ever encountered.

When I went to Wellesley College in the fall of 1930, I anticipated joining a community of scholars, classmates who would share my new intellectual interests, professors who would challenge me — and all this in an idyllic country setting only half an hour from Boston. The campus *was* beautiful: lofty oaks and elms, rolling lawns, ivy-covered Gothic buildings, and a lake that held out a promise of swimming and boating. All else was a disappointment. Instead of Dalton's Jewish debutantes I was now surrounded by WASP achievers who had spent their prep school years cramming for the College Boards. I had dreamed of dormitory bull sessions that would range from art to literature to politics. There were bull sessions, but the main topic of conversation was boys. I was the only girl in my freshman dorm who subscribed to the *New York Times*.

Close to My Heart

The ethnic mix took some getting used to. I had known that Wellesley had a ten percent quota for Jewish students, a policy instituted in all Ivy League colleges in the 1920s, when the grandchildren of the great wave of Eastern European immigrants were ready for higher education and admissions officers feared that a "foreign element" might "overrun" the colleges. At Wellesley, Jewish origin was ascertained by the application, which asked for "religious affiliation" and "mother's maiden name," but Vassar, where Alice went two years later, required a personal interview. Proficient at reading upside down, she saw the admissions officer's description of herself: "a clever-looking Jewess," a phrase that upset my parents.

When two classmates did a head count, they discovered that Wellesley took its quota literally. Out of four hundred ten freshmen, forty-one were Jewish (and four black). Although we were scattered through the dormitories, several of us were assigned rooms on the same second-floor corridor at Dower, a small dorm at the edge of the campus, while a lone black girl lived on the first floor. We ate our meals in Stone, a larger residential hall, taking seats at any table without fear of being unwelcome. This was not true for our black dormitory mate, however. When she sat down, three girls who came from Baltimore pointedly rose and moved to another table. The rest of us remained seated, talking loudly to cover up the affront. To my lifelong regret, I

49

did not take the obvious next step—to walk back to Dower with the girl and make friends. Black people were strangers to me, and although I wanted to reach out I did not know how to do it. She must have been a remarkably strong young woman; after enduring four years at Wellesley she went on to become a doctor. I wish I had known her.

My only direct encounter with anti-Semitism was in Bible class. Two years of Bible—historical analysis, not religion—were required. I might have found the class interesting had not the professor called on me so frequently. "Now, Miss Dannenberg, tell us how the Jews celebrate Passover—Purim—or Chanukah— and how it relates to the passage we are reading." It was embarrassing to be singled out as the only Jew in the class, doubly so because I never knew the answers to her questions and feared that my classmates would think I was trying to conceal my Jewishness. Looking back, I have sometimes wondered if I had not been overly sensitive. I held this charitable view until the 1980s, when a Jewish professor who had been denied tenure in Wellesley's Religion Department uncovered some shocking anti-Semitic correspondence between a member of the department and a former college president. Threatened with a lawsuit, the Religion Department offered the professor tenure, making him the first Jewish tenured faculty member in the 108-year history of the department. A more sensitive administration initiated a program to eliminate anti-Semitism at Wellesley.*

Bible was not the only disappointing course. Spec Op and Dalton had not prepared me for classes in which the professors lectured and the student parroted back the information on exams. The most talked-of course was Freshman Hygiene. All four hundred one of us filed into the college's largest lecture hall to learn how our bodies worked. Upperclassmen had warned that girls fainted when the professor showed slides illustrating the fertilization of an egg by a sperm. Perhaps our class was sturdier than its predecessors; no one passed out when the professor dryly described coitus, omitting the best-kept secret of our youth: that intercourse produced pleasure as well as problems. Birth control, of course, was never mentioned; the laws of the Commonwealth of Massachusetts forbade the dissemination of such information.

Homosexuality was also omitted from Freshman Hygiene. At home, when I asked my mother what a lesbian was, she had given me a characteristically humorless reply: "I don't know. I'm not that kind of woman." The publication of *The Well of Loneliness* by Radcliffe Hall had offered some enlightenment, and I suspected that two girls on the first floor of Dower

---

The Jewish Advocate, September 29, 1983.

were "that kind." Since homosexuals were liable to expulsion, I never broached the taboo topic.

Other required courses included Freshman Composition and Speech, where a teacher with a broad New England accent (she said to-mah-to; I said to-may-to) labeled my accent "Brooklynese" and took me to task accordingly. Botany was the one course that I was enthusiastic about. Not only did I find answers to the questions I had long been asking, but I was introduced to Darwin's mind-expanding theory. The professor was careful to emphasize "theory." The Scopes trial, in which a Tennessee high-school teacher had been convicted for teaching evolution, was only five years behind us; there were creationists everywhere, even at Wellesley. I enjoyed the field trips—to see the glass flowers at the Agassiz Museum at Harvard, to collect seaweed at a nearby beach—and I can still evoke the humid fragrance of the greenhouse where we planted seeds and recorded their development.

The department was small and friendly. Professors invited us to doughnuts and cider at their homes and held a contest each spring to see who could spot the earliest flowers. Not only did I win the contest, receiving as a prize a book titled *How to Tell the Birds from the Flowers*, but I had A's in both Introductory Botany and the course I took my sophomore year. Yet when I told my professor that I planned to major in Botany, she advised against it. "The only jobs for women botanists are in landscape gardening, and you draw too poorly for that," she said. Had I been more persistent, I might have asked about the academic world, where she, after all, was employed. And had she been more forthcoming, she might have warned of the difficulty women scientists faced in gaining admission to graduate school and the near impossibility of finding jobs afterward. Perhaps the big fact that she refrained from telling me was that no college would appoint a Jew to its faculty. Totally ignorant of opportunities for women in other professions—I had never met a woman lawyer or doctor—I accepted the professor's advice. Being a botanist has always been one of my wish-I'd-beens.

I was still trying to decide on a major when I joined the College Press Board, the undergraduate group that publicized Wellesley activities in city newspapers. When the *New York Sun* paid me $2 for an article, my father framed a photocopy of the check and hung it on his office wall. Other Press Board members planned to be journalists, but even though I had just read Virginia Woolf's *A Room of One's Own* I did not picture myself as a writer. In the too quick way in which I formed judgments I concluded that the English Department was narrow, overly interested in dotting "i's" and crossing "t's." Therefore I decided to follow in David's footsteps and major in Philosophy.

"Philosophy!" my parents and their friends exclaimed. "What good will that do you?" "I am not going to college in order to get a job, but to become a well-rounded cultured human being," I would loftily reply. Sometimes I quoted John Keats: "'Beauty is truth, truth beauty'—that is all 'ye know on earth, and all ye need to know." So there I was at eighteen with "art for art's sake" as my guiding principle. But the year was 1932. The stock market crash, which had at first seemed a local disaster, had initiated a world wide depression. When I went home on weekends, men in frayed serge suits stood behind upended crates at street corners on Broadway, selling apples for a nickel apiece. On Riverside Drive and in Central Park families lived in shacks built of tarpaper and flattened tin cans, called Hoovervilles in honor of our ineffectual president. Downtown, men queued up at unemployment offices and soup kitchens, hoping for handouts. Others demonstrated at City Hall and were knocked down by club-swinging policemen.

When I returned to Wellesley after spring vacation, the tranquil campus was jarring. Elm flowers dangled from the trees, crocuses and daffodils bloomed, and the college president, her white hair perfectly marcelled, drove along the road in her electric car, a symbol of an earlier time. When Norman Thomas, the handsome, silver-haired head of the Socialist Party, came to lecture on the depression, students almost mobbed him afterward in their eagerness to shake his hand. The following week there was a rush to buy knitting needles and wool. "What are you doing?" I asked a classmate. "I'm knitting for the poor." she replied.

Suddenly I was overwhelmed by Wellesley's insularity. I decided to transfer to Barnard at the end of sophomore year. Sister college to Columbia University, Barnard was at 116th Street and Broadway. Its campus lacked the beauty of Wellesley's, but it was in New York City, part of the real world. My parents welcomed my decision. Alice was going to Vassar in the fall, and by living at home and commuting to classes on the subway, I would put less strain on the family budget.

David, who had graduated from college and was job hunting, was often at our house that summer, and Dad invited him to spend a Saturday at Broadmoor Country Club. David was well versed in literature and philosophy but hopelessly ignorant of men's fashions. Eager to do the right thing, he went to considerable trouble to outfit himself with a pair of knickerbockers for the occasion. Knickers had been correct golfing attire in the 1920s but they had not been seen at a Westchester club for years. The four of us spent an uncomfortable day at the club, where every man save "that Dannenberg girl's date" wore slacks. The following morning Dad gravely informed me, "He's not our kind."

I did not, of course, let my parents' judgment influence me. The incident seemed unimportant, as I was caught up in new interests at Barnard. In the study hall where day students gathered, girls urged me to sign up for Anthropology and Government. I had never heard the word "anthropology" and thus missed a chance to study under a youthful Margaret Mead. However, I managed to audit Professor Raymond Moley's Government classes. Moley headed Franklin D. Roosevelt's "Brain Trust," the group of college professors who put together the economic program that became known as the New Deal. Commuting from Washington to Barnard, he captivated his students with anecdotes about FDR, "Wee Willie" Woodin, Secretary of the Treasury, and other cabinet members.

I was only peripherally aware of many changes around the world. A month before Roosevelt's inauguration, Adolf Hitler was appointed chancellor of Germany. David and I watched newsreels at Loews 83rd Street Theatre, where the audience tittered at his Charlie Chaplin moustache and jerky oratorical style. His anti-Semitic mouthings posed little threat, we concluded. We also viewed with equanimity FDR's recognition of the Soviet Union in November 1933. Neither of us paid much attention to the socialist experiment, except to hope that now we would be able to see such great Russian films as *Potemkin* and *Ten Days That Shook the World*. Similarly, our interest in art rather than politics brought us to Rockefeller Center to watch Diego Rivera at work. Twenty-five-year-old Nelson

Rockefeller, a grandson of John D., had commissioned the famed Mexican artist to decorate the walls of the new RCA building. By the time David and I went to see him—a huge, overalled figure high above us on a scaffold—the revolutionary theme of his murals was apparent. Panels showed police breaking up an unemployment demonstration and May Day at Red Square with hammers and sickles waving. After Rivera gave a labor leader the features of Vladimir Lenin, Rockefeller ordered changes. When Rivera refused, he was fired and the mural chipped off the walls.

I enjoyed every moment of the controversy, which culminated in an E. B. White poem in the *New Yorker*, with a purported quote from young Nelson:

> "And though your art I dislike to hamper
> I owe a little to God and Gramper.
> And, after all,
> It's my wall."
> "We'll see if it is," said Rivera.

But it did not occur to me to join the picket line in front of the RCA building. It was not until I broke up with David later that year that I began to question the world around me.

By 1934 the New Deal had not cured the nation's ills. Millions were still unemployed. Perhaps something was basically wrong with the capitalist system. My Philosophy classes had carried me from Heraclitus to Hegel, but no professor had mentioned Karl Marx. The closest we came to contemporary life was a senior course titled "Radical and Conservative Morals," where we read Thorstein Veblen's *Theory of the Leisure Class* and Prince Peter Kropotkin's *Memoirs of a Revolutionist*, but never mentioned the Soviet Union.

I was too early by a year or two for the militant student movement but caught a glimpse of its beginnings. Once when the contract of a radical professor was not renewed I attended a protest meeting on the Columbia campus where the main speaker was Heywood Broun, formerly of the Algonquin, now founder of the American Newspaper Guild. After he defended the fired professor, he ducked behind the massive statue of Alma Mater for a nip from his pocket flask. I felt more involved when Ad Reinhart, the boy sitting next to me in a Music Appreciation class, drew a cartoon satirizing Nicholas Murray Butler, president of the university, who opposed a federal child labor law. Reinhart's cartoon showing Butler clubbing small children was rejected by the college humor magazine but published on the front page of the *Columbia Daily Spectator* and in several city newspapers. (Reinhart's political cartoons later appeared in *New Masses* and *Masses and Mainstream*; he also became a leader of the Abstract Expressionist school and was noted for painting black-on-black canvases.)

However, my real introduction to the left came when Alice returned from Vassar one weekend singing:

> Fly higher and higher and higher
> Our emblem is the Soviet Star
> And every propeller is roaring RED FRONT
> Defending the USSR.

She and a half dozen of her friends had formed a branch of the Young Communist League. The Vassar YCL in no way resembled the stereotypes of Reds portrayed in the Hearst press. Bright, well-dressed, attractive, its members majored in English, Art History, Mathematics, wrote for the college paper, and had date-filled weekends in New York. But they boycotted silk stockings after Japan invaded Manchuria, picketed a factory in support of striking workers, and sent delegates to a YCL convention. And they read, or at least carried around, pamphlets on communism and socialism. I still have "A Handbook of Marxism," a collection of the classic writings of Marx and Engels that one Vassar YCLer gave me as a hostess present after she stayed at our house for weekends.

When I asked two of these women, now octogenarians, why they had become Young Communists in 1934, they replied with some embarrassment, "It was in the air." It was in the air on 116th Street, too, but I did not learn of a Columbia-Barnard YCL until two decades later, when James Wechsler, then editor of the *New York Evening Post,* testified about it to Senator Joseph McCarthy's investigating committee. On May 1, 1934, I was sufficiently curious to take the subway to Union Square where, standing at the edge of the crowd, I listened to the speakers at the May Day rally.

The swan song of my art-for-art's-sake period came that summer, when Alice and I made a long-planned trip to Europe. She was majoring in art history and I had taken a number of art courses, so our goal was to visit museums in France, Italy, and Great Britain. Admirers of Roger Fry, the Bloomsbury critic who had introduced the Post-Impressionists to England, we subscribed to his theory of "significant form," lifting our eyebrows when people uttered that deathless cliché, "I don't know anything about art, but I know what I like." We thought we knew a lot about art and what Roger Fry liked. While we tracked down Giottos, Titians, and Michelangelos, politics occasionally intruded. Having read George Seldes' *Sawdust Caesar,* a critical study of Mussolini, we made fun of his blackshirted troops—in English—when we saw them in public places. We were in Rome when Austria's Chancellor Dollfuss was assassinated by Nazis. Feeling a momentary chill, we hunted for a copy of the Paris *Herald* to learn the details, but did not of course recognize it as a significant step toward World War II. At summer's end, Alice returned to Vassar and I started looking for a job.

CHAPTER

4

Job hunting in 1934 was discouraging. With more than ten million still unemployed, there was little likelihood that a new college graduate could find work. What did I hope to do, anyway? Although I had some slight facility with words, I never seriously thought of writing as a career. Nor did I want to teach or stay at home to perfect my culinary skills until Mr. Right came along. In the past, liberal arts graduates had found jobs in publishing, but the few publishers who had survived the crash were not hiring. The only skill I had picked up during my college years came from a business school on Broadway where, after classes at Barnard, I had learned touch typing and the rudiments of shorthand. Secretarial jobs, however, were rarely listed in the want ads.

With Mother as unwilling as ever to have me at home, I hunted for volunteer work. The Frick Collection of paintings and sculpture was to open as a museum on Fifth Avenue in 1935. I typed catalogue cards for the curators and wrote short art reviews for a publication of the College Art Association. Through the new graduates' grapevine, I learned that the *New York Times* and *Evening Sun* occasionally gave out books for review. Once a week or so I traveled to the West Side to call at the offices of the book review editors. Once a month or so, an editor would point a finger at the pile of books on the far corner of his desk and wearily say, "Take one." These were minor novels that might or might not be reviewed, depending on space. I treated each one as if it were *Jane Eyre* or *Wuthering Heights*. If it lacked literary merit—and it usually did—I said so sharply. Once Faith Baldwin, known as a circulating library novelist, complained of my harsh review in the *Times*. She said that she wrote night and day in order to support a large, needy family. Further, the plot that I called "mediocre" was the true story of her parents' and grandparents' lives. I winced when I read her letter, glad that she did not know of my youth and inexperience, but never considered lowering my literary standards. In the notebook in which Mother pasted clippings of my writings, there are eight or nine reviews from 1934–35. Paid by the word, each earned about $20, my major cash income for the period.

Reading scripts for movie companies was another source of income. The New York offices of Warner Brothers and Twentieth-Century Fox screened new novels before forwarding them to the West Coast. Readers were employed to write detailed synopses so that Hollywood moguls could learn the plots without taking time to go through the books. Although we were paid only $25 for close to a week's work, there were so many applicants that I considered myself lucky if I got a book a month.

While reading romances for pay I was also reading novels about unemployed miners, steelworkers, and dispossessed farmers, and sharing this interest in the new popular field of proletarian literature with Tommy, a graduate student in history at City College. Tommy was an eminently acceptable young man who lived with his family in the Beresford, an elegant apartment house on Central Park West and 81st Street. My parents had known his for many years. Since we were both mavericks in their circle, where girls married young and boys went into their father's business, our mothers had decided to bring us together. They did not know that Tommy was a budding Marxist who gave me a copy of Charles and Mary Beard's *Rise of American Civilization* for my twenty-first birthday and brought me to a weekly discussion group in an apartment on 113th Street where City College graduate students and instructors met to analyze Karl Marx's *Capital* and the philosophy of dialectical materialism. They discussed, and I listened, for I was not prepared to speak on surplus value, primitive accumulation, or the use value of commodities, topics with which they all seemed familiar. Perhaps it was just as well that I was silent; one member of the group, a skinny, freckle-faced youngster, turned informer several years later when the Rapp-Coudert Committee, a state legislative body, investigated communist activity in New York schools. He fingered members of the discussion group as Reds, cutting short several promising academic careers.

Over endless cups of coffee after the discussions concluded, Tommy and I weighed capitalism and socialism. FDR's New Deal was endlessly improvising, trying different tactics to shorten the depression, but unemployment remained high, farm income low, and evictions a daily occurrence. In contrast, the Soviet Union had a bold Five-Year Plan, which called for building dams and power stations and raising crops on vast collective farms. We were serious seekers after the truth that winter, determined to find a meaning to life that went beyond the pursuit of money—money for some and poverty for others. It did not take us long to ask the obvious question. If Karl Marx was right and socialism was the wave of the future, what were we doing on the sidelines?

In the United States, a small Communist Party was taking leadership in organizing hunger marches, stopping evictions, and organizing unions. No one we knew belonged to the Party, or admitted it, anyway. Party membership was hardly a plus on a job application. But when we looked in the Manhattan telephone book we found several listings. The national headquarters of the Communist Party was on 12th Street, but there were local addresses too, including one on 81st Street, only two blocks from where we both lived.

Without taking the time to weigh the consequences—and what consequences could there be for twenty-one-year-olds supported in comfort by their parents?—we went to a shabby brownstone off Columbus Avenue the next afternoon. In response to our knock, a soft voice bade us "Come in" and a man introduced himself as Sam Brown, district organizer of the Communist Party on the Upper West Side. He was middle-aged, affable, low-key, his only distinguishing characteristic a slight lisp so that we privately spoke of him as "Sam Bwown." He listened gravely when we told him we wanted to join the Communist Party, questioned us briefly, then picked up a pen and matter-of-factly enrolled us.

Although he asked for our names and addresses he did not write them down, advising us instead to choose pseudonyms—Party names—so that if the FBI penetrated the files at 12th Street (they did), the agents would not be able to identify us. I chose a truncated version of my name, something like "Dorothy Dane." For some years when the CP held its annual re-registration, I answered to this name, but after a time it was dropped and my real name used instead. Tommy and I paid modest initiation fees, while Brown explained that we would meet every Tuesday evening at a member's house. He gave us the address of the first meeting and that was that.

We did not receive membership cards, then or later. For sixty years I have read of "card-carrying members of the Communist Party," but I never met such a person. Except once during World War II, which I'll tell about later, I never saw a Party card. Nor did I join a "cell." Tommy and I became members of a neighborhood branch; later I belonged to a shop unit. I'm prepared to believe that there were cells somewhere, and perhaps membership cards, but they were outside of my experience.

In fact, joining the Communist Party, which had sounded like a big adventure, was disappointingly tame. Meetings were held in modest apartments near our homes. Members were a bit older than we: salesmen, teachers, clerks, some unemployed. We were the only ones still living with our families. The meetings followed a prescribed routine. After the chairman read announcements of forthcoming rallies and fundraisers, a "literature agent" displayed the latest pamphlets, a few Soviet books and *USSR in Construction*, an oversized picture magazine that showed buxom collective farm women riding tractors or pitchforking bales of hay. Purchasing the pamphlets on current topics was mandatory. They cost a nickel or a dime, and people who didn't have the money promised to pay next time; recordkeeping was casual. We also had to buy the particular Marxist classic that the branch was studying: *Socialism: Utopian and Scientific*, by Engels, *State and Revolution* by Lenin, or *Dialectical and Historical Materialism* by Joseph Stalin. Published in paper by International Publishers, these cost thirty or forty cents. Since we spent months on one pamphlet, the expense of "literature" was not onerous.

The discussion itself was rather low level. Usually one or two verbal people did all the talking while the rest of us listened. Afterward a place was chosen for the next meeting, always on Tuesday. Across the country from New York to California, Communist branches met on Tuesday nights. Perhaps someone on 12th Street had decided that it gave a feeling of solidarity to think of thousands getting together on the same night; perhaps it simplified the organizing calendar. Once a fellow traveler (the accepted phrase for sympathizer) told me that when he wanted to know if someone belonged to the Party he invited him to dinner on successive Tuesdays; if he was busy repeatedly, it was a sure sign of membership. Even in a later period, when Party members were security-conscious and FBI agents were everywhere, Tuesday remained the official meeting night.

On Saturday nights there was usually a cause party, which we were expected to attend. The socials raised money to free Tom Mooney, the nation's oldest political prisoner, or to defend the Scottsboro boys, nine black youngsters who had been pulled off a train in Scottsboro, Alabama in 1931 and charged with raping two white girls. Although there was no evidence to support the charge, an Alabama jury found them guilty and sentenced all but the youngest to die in the electric chair. The Communist Party and its legal arm, the International Labor Defense, was the first organization to come forward to fight for their freedom. Eventually the case was carried to the Supreme Court and the court of public opinion at home and abroad, but it was not until 1950 that the last of the "boys" was set free. Reading their saga in the *Daily Worker* was my introduction to the plight of black people in the South. Paying 75 cents for a highball and a handful of pretzels and joining in the chant: "The Scottsboro boys must not die / Workers led by the ILD / Will set them free" seemed a small price to right so terrible a wrong.

One could hardly call these prosaic meetings and socials manning the barricades. Tommy and I were both disappointed and relieved that so little was required of us. The closest we came to action that winter was when the building service employees union went on strike. With scabs manning the elevators at 118 West 79th Street, I walked up and down twelve flights of stairs, probably the only tenant in the building to do so. Breathless and virtuous, I brought coffee to the men on the picket line, who seemed more embarrassed than pleased.

Close to My Heart

Bored with the fruitless search for work, I was grateful in the spring of 1935 when a Vassar YCLer suggested that I volunteer at *New Theatre Magazine*. The organ of the League of Workers Theatre, the magazine had grown from a mimeographed bulletin to an illustrated monthly that covered "revolutionary" theatre, film, and dance. The Workers Theatre movement which had sprung up in the early days of the depression, put on short skits that could be performed in union halls or on picket lines. But by 1935 revolutionary theater had become respectable. Motion pictures were still concerned with boy-meets-girl; radio was perfecting the soap opera; but the theater was a major force in shaping and presenting ideas. At the Theatre Guild, Broadway audiences watched John Wexley's play about the Scottsboro boys, *They Shall Not Die*. On 14th Street, the newly organized Theatre Union put on *Stevedore* and *Peace on Earth*, plays with working-class content, while the Group Theatre, a collective of actors, writers, and directors, had its first spectacular success with *Waiting for Lefty*, by young Clifford Odets. Prizewinner in a *New Theatre* playwriting contest, *Lefty*, a play about the murder of a union organizer, was playing in cities across the country; it had even been banned in Boston.

The *New Theatre*'s editor was Herbert Kline, a personable and energetic young man whose main job was raising money to keep the publication afloat. Once when the printer would wait no longer for his pay, I brought Herb home to dinner. It was a reflection of the times that he charmed my father into lending the magazine $500. Astonishing as this was, it was even more astonishing when Herb repaid the debt some months later. Most of *New Theatre*'s creditors were not as lucky. Second in command was Molly Day Thacher, a graduate of Vassar and the Yale School of Drama. Listed on the masthead as Drama editor, she put out the magazine and worked with Odets and Irwin Shaw, another young playwright whose anti-war play *Bury the Dead* was a left theater sensation a year later. Married to Elia Kazan, the Group Theatre actor who played the leading role in *Lefty*, she was the first capable and confident woman I had ever met. At first she put me to work sorting mail and retyping articles; later she taught me to paste up the dummy of the magazine and to proofread its final pages, skills that I would often use in later years.

In the months that I spent at *New Theatre*, I was introduced to the exciting cultural developments of an exciting period. I saw striking documentary photographs by Paul Strand, Dorothea Lange, and others that were on exhibit at the Film and Photo League, went to modern dance recitals where Martha Graham and her star pupils performed *Uprising* and *Scottsboro*, and even saw a revolutionary Punch and Judy show, which ended with Punch vowing to fight "to use our might." Most important in the development of my own understanding was a special Negro issue of the magazine, which made me aware of the talents of black artists and the strangling effect of Jim Crow. Paul Robeson, whose magnificent performance in *Show Boat* in the 1920s had won him worldwide renown, still had to ride in freight elevators and sleep in ramshackle boarding houses when he toured in the United States. Interviewed for *New Theatre* while in Moscow, the article about him was titled "I Breathe Freely." Another article introduced me to poet and playwright Langston Hughes, who reported on the Washington, D.C. production of *Green Pastures*. Although the play was based on black folklore and had an all-black cast, no black people were permitted in the audience.

Since the magazine was always behind schedule, I sometimes worked late. On those occasions Molly insisted on driving me home in her Ford coupe, even though she lived in a different part of the city. Once when I got out of the car at 2:00 A.M. I looked up at the facade of the apartment building to see a row of lights on the twelfth floor. I knew what that meant. When I let myself into the apartment, two agitated parents descended on me. "Where have you been? We've called the police. We've called the hospitals." (Had they really?) The contrast between my life and Molly's could hardly have been sharper. I was almost twenty-two years old, but as long as I lived at home I was still a child. With an income that rarely topped $25 a month, I could hardly rent a place of my own. Besides, did I really want to give up having meals cooked, clothes washed, and beds made for me?

One perk that I gladly accepted was my allowance. That summer Alice and I went abroad again for a month in England. Although we devoted many hours to the National Gallery and the Tate, we were no longer exclusively art students. We toured England by bus, enjoying the chalk cliffs of Dover and high tea in an Oxford boarding house. In London, where we had letters of introduction to progressive theater people, including a serious young actor named John Gielgud, we spent much of our time at the theater and backstage.

We traveled on the *Veendam* and *Volendam*, or first-class ships of the Holland America Line that ordinarily took ten days for the Atlantic crossing. The trip home was longer because of a storm at sea. After we had caught up with our sleep we were entertained by a German newspaperman who was smitten with Alice. Curt Reiss—short, dark, charming—had been a journalist in Berlin until all Jews were fired. He had escaped from Germany, he told us, by skiing across the Alps in evening clothes. He even offered to show us the scars on his back caused by Nazi beatings. Although I was skeptical of some of Curt's tales, his anti-Nazi credentials proved to be genuine. In New York he worked as a correspondent for *Paris Soir* and lived near us in the West 70s. There we met many of the German intellectuals who were seeking refuge in the United States. We had long ago given up thinking of Hitler as a comic figure. When we met Curt's friends, such people as Hans Eisler, the composer, and his wife, and Rudolph Breda, editor of *The Brown Book of Hitler Terror*, the first sickening catalogue of Hitler brutality, we felt in a direct way the evil that the Nazis represented.

Curt and his friends were not the only refugees that Alice and I encountered in those years. Frances, the red-cheeked curly-haired woman who had long been Mother's housekeeper and our confidante, was an American citizen of Czech birth. On her days off, she went to the Czech Workers Club in Yorkville, meeting such Czech expatriates as Voskovich and Werick, former stars of Prague's music halls, and the noted composer Jaroslav Ježek. Already ill with the tuberculosis that would claim his life, Ježek fell in love with Frances, and they married. We spent many evenings with the Czechs and their families while they tried to translate their songs and jokes into an idiom that we could follow and we endeavored to help them solve some of the practical problems of living in New York. Frances continued to work for Mother after Ježek's death but later retired to Czechoslovakia, where she was honored as the widow of the nation's beloved composer.

When I went back to *New Theatre* after the British trip, my name was on the masthead as an Associate, along with Muriel Rukeyser, who had just published her first book of poems; Jay Leyda, head of the Museum of Modern Art's new Film Library; and others far more distinguished than I. I was listed as "Dorothy Dannen," following the tradition of changing and shortening foreign-sounding names. In the 1920s and 1930s, there were no Ginsburgs, Wallskys, or Feinsteins on book jackets or theater programs. On the mastheads of left publications, Irwin Granich became Mike Gold; Louis Fraina, Lewis Corey; and Ilya Greenberg, Philip Rahv. Contributors to the *New Masses* and *Partisan Review* sounded as Anglo-Saxon as those who wrote for the *Saturday Evening Post*. This relinquishing of birth names was part of the melting pot process. The children of immigrants wanted to sound as American—and non-Jewish—as possible. The old mastheads are interesting to compare with the front page of today's newspaper which, as I write, is evenly divided between the exploits of Ms. Lipinski, Olympic skating star, and Ms. Lewinsky, former White House intern.

Answering an ad in the *Times* in the fall of 1935, I finally got a job, a real job paying $15 a week. I was hired as a secretary/salesperson in a Madison Avenue art gallery and antiques store. My boss, a plump Jewish matron, showed me her objets d'art proudly, pointing particularly to two paintings, one by Rembrandt and one by Vermeer, she said. However, she needed certificates to prove their authenticity. I typed a letter asking a well-known art professor to come to her gallery to examine the paintings. The expert arrived the following week, studied the pictures, and dictated a statement declaring that one was indeed a Rembrandt, the other a Vermeer. After he left with a $75 honorarium in his wallet, my boss winked broadly, confirming my suspicion that he knew and she knew and I knew that the paintings were at best from the schools of the famous artists, if not more recent copies. Uncomfortable as this made me feel, it was not nearly as upsetting as the moment soon afterward when she pulled me on her lap and began to fondle me. I left as quickly as I could.

Almost immediately I found work on the *Art News*, a weekly publication that was written and edited by three women. The editor and assistant editor covered the major exhibitions, while for a salary of $12.50 a week, I reviewed the smaller galleries and wrote a column headed "Paris Notes," based on English-language summaries clipped from French newspapers. Once when the editor was ill I reviewed an exhibition of paintings by John Marin and received a warm note from the great Alfred Stieglitz praising my discernment. That was the height of my career as art critic, because soon afterward the magazine was sold; the new publisher replaced the three of us with an all-male staff.

Back working at *New Theatre*, I heard that there were jobs on the arts projects. The New Deal had been putting unemployed people to work building roads, cleaning parks, repairing bridges. Under pressure from such white-collar unions as the Newspaper Guild, Actors Equity, and the Musicians Union, the Works Progress Administration was launching projects for needy artists, writers, and musicians as well. Limited at first to those on home relief, hiring procedures were eventually broadened to include any unemployed artist or writer. This meant that I could apply for a job even though I lived at home with my parents.

CHAPTER

5

On a cold February morning in 1936, I took the subway downtown, heading for the loft building in the East 30s where the Federal Writers' Project was housed. I had dressed carefully: a pastel, square-necked sweater, matching skirt, and a strand of pearls, the Ivy League uniform, and I carried a notebook containing the reviews I had written. The job interviews were conducted in a dusty, drafty room empty of furniture save for a desk and two chairs. Applicants stood in line nervously inching forward as one, then a second and third were heard. Surreptitiously I looked at the others, who seemed older and seedier than I. Perhaps I had dressed too well for the occasion. The man behind me, a saturnine-looking character, suddenly began to whistle the "Internationale." I froze, sure that he was an agent provocateur. If I showed by so much as the blink of an eye that I recognized the song I would be dismissed, if not denounced, as a communist. Standing ramrod straight, I was careful not to make eye contact with anyone.

At last it was my turn. The woman behind the desk skimmed through my notebook, asked briefly about my work experience and current joblessness, then gave me a slip of paper directing me to report to the Writers' Project office, a floor above, on Monday next. Hours 8:30 to 4:30. She was filling three job categories: supervisors who were paid the princely sum of $27.50 a week, editors, $23.86, and legmen $21.67. She had classified me as an editor. Maybe the sweater and pearls had impressed her.

Monday morning found me at the sparsely furnished headquarters of the New York City Writers' Project. The offices, on several floors, were huge bullpens divided by strategically placed desks and one shoulder-high partition, which gave project director Orrick Johns a minimum of privacy. Most of the staff were working on a guidebook of New York, which would cover history, folklore, sports, and the traditional sights-to-see. (*New York City Guide* and *New York Panorama* were published in 1938–39.) Smaller groups were investigating the city's ethnic minorities; still others were compiling a bibliography of the motion pictures, and a "Who's Who in the Zoo." The Yiddish writers, bearded men wearing yarmulkes, were the most visible. They were completing a study, *The Jewish Landsmanschaften of New York*, still a standard reference in its field. Seldom seen were the aristocrats of the project, the handful of creative writers who worked at home and came in on Fridays to bring their week's output and pick up their paychecks. These included Muriel Rukeyser, Edward Dahlberg, Claude McKay, and young Richard Wright, whose short stories I had been reading in *New Masses* and who had started his novel *Native Son* while he was on WPA.

I soon had a nodding acquaintance with Maxwell Bodenheim, a Greenwich Village poet of an earlier generation, who spent most of his time in neighborhood saloons. At weekend parties, I met Eli Siegel, the man who had whistled the "Internationale." The winner of a poetry prize for *Hot Afternoons I Have Seen in Montana*, he was known for his booming rendition of Vachel Lindsay's "The Congo." Among the older writers was Frank Shay, newspaperman and raconteur, who had written such books as *Judge Lynch* and *My Pious Friends and Drunken Companions* and had been a co-founder of the Provincetown Players on Cape Cod, where Eugene O'Neill's first plays were produced. Frank was editing *Almanac for New Yorkers*, an anthology of poems and stories which became the Writers' Project's first publication.

For the most part, I found a place among people close to my age, tyro writers whose careers had been put on hold by the depression. They were the sons and daughters of Russian immigrants who had come to the United States after the aborted revolution of 1905. Many had grown up in the Co-ops, cooperative apartment houses in the Bronx built in the 1920s. At lunch in the back room of the corner saloon (the only inexpensive restaurant in the neighborhood) and at dinner in Stewart's Cafeteria on 14th Street, I strained to follow as they talked of Wobblies and 1905ers, Mother Jones and Mother Bloor, Joe Hill, and Jack London. Almost without exception, my parents would have classified them as "not our kind." I found them wise and witty, knowledgeable about a hundred topics that were new to me.

I was assigned to the Historical Records Survey, initially under the Writers' Project umbrella but later administered directly from Washington. The survey's goal was to locate old records in borough halls, courtrooms, and libraries, and to transcribe the land deeds, slave sales, and colonial reports that they contained. The purpose was laudable but the execution flawed. People with no training in historical research were assigned to copy difficult-to-read, archaically spelled manuscripts. Most of us tried our best, but the rote copying was boring and the margin for error great.

In my first week on the project I joined the Writers Union, excited beyond measure to be a part of the burgeoning union movement. The passage of the National Labor Relations Act a year earlier had for the first time affirmed labor's right to organize. Workers in auto, steel, textiles, often led by communists, were deserting the American Federation of Labor's craft unions for the Congress of Industrial Organizations—the CIO. Even white-collar workers were flocking to the Newspaper Guild, Teachers Union, and Federation of Architects, Engineers, Chemists and Technicians.

Soon after joining the union, I was elected secretary. As I sat on the platform taking notes, it never occurred to me that secretary was the traditional woman's job that left the men in policy-making positions. Nor did I question how I came to be elected after such a short time on the project. I saw my election as a sign that my fellow workers liked me. For the first time since Spec Op, I was with people who shared my interests and didn't care if I was the first to open a door or had unfashionable hair. People invited me to join them at lunch and dinner; there were times when a man attempted to fondle me, incidents that today might be called sexual harassment but that I found flattering.

A more cynical person would have guessed that my election came about so quickly because I had been transferred to the communist shop unit of the Writers' Project. Had a poll of project workers been taken, Democrats would have been in the majority, with even a few Republicans signing in. But the communists were the best organized and vociferous union members, battling for control over Socialists, Trotskyists, and smaller left groups.

Believing, as the song said, "The union makes us strong," I became a self-appointed spokesperson on

Historical Records. I asked for traveling time and car-
fare for those who had to go to the Bronx or Brooklyn
and, in my cocky way, criticized errors of transcrip-
tion. I was flexing my muscles and feeling the strength
of the union, but I grossly underestimated management's power.

The director of Historical Records, a rigid woman
who reminded me of one of my Wellesley professors,
called me to her desk one morning to tell me that I was
being transferred. On Monday next, I was to report to
the Triborough Bridge Authority to join a project that
counted the number of cars entering and leaving the
city.

I was stunned. The Writers' Project was the best
thing that had ever happened to me. I could hardly
wait to come to work each morning, to rub elbows
with journalists, novelists, poets, people who made
their living—or hoped to—with their typewriters. As
soon as I learned of the transfer I sought out Philip
Sterling, a member of the union grievance committee.
A twenty-eight-year-old newspaperman, Phil had
worked on the *Bronx Home News* and *Staten Island
Advance*, Si Newhouse's first paper, until the depression forced cutbacks. His parents had been Bundists
(Jewish Socialists) in Russia. His father had been
briefly exiled to Siberia for taking part in a May Day
demonstration. Phil had grown up in Cleveland,
attending Sunday school at the Socialist Labor

Lyceum; and on one momentous occasion, he had presented a bouquet of roses to Eugene V. Debs, the Socialist leader. While I was singing "Onward Christian Soldiers" and following the adventures of *Stover at Yale*, he was learning Wobbly songs and reading *The Iron Heel* and *Pelle the Conqueror*. During the darkest years of the Depression, he had worked as a home relief investigator and had written for *New Masses* and *New Theatre* in his spare time. One of the first to join the Writers' Project, he was a supervisor on the Motion Picture Bibliography. Dark-haired and intense, he had blue-green eyes and a ready smile.

At the end of the work day, Phil and I walked to 23rd Street, where he arranged to use the office of an electricians' union local. Taking over a battered desk and typewriter, he quickly composed a leaflet, then read it to me for my approval. To say that I fell in love as I turned the handle of a rickety mimeograph machine sounds like a skit from a 1930s musical comedy, but it would not be far from the truth.

We met at the doorway of the project at 8:15 the next morning and handed out the leaflets, headed DOROTHY DANNENBERG TRANSFERRED. Although embarrassed by the notoriety, I was pleased at the number of people who offered their support. Later that morning the union grievance committee met with Orrick Johns. A 1920s bohemian and former communist, Johns rendered a Solomon-like judgment. The Historical Records director could transfer me if my behavior troubled her, but how would I like to join the staff of the Motion Picture Bibliography? Barely able to conceal a smile, I said "Fine."

Although the movies had been around for forty years, no one had yet attempted to examine and organize the growing number of books and periodicals devoted to films. Harold Leonard, a Harvard M.A. with some Hollywood experience, had drawn up a plan for a bibliography that would digest more than ten thousand books and articles, plus a directory of film reviews from 1896 to 1936, and an index to movie-related topics, from Griffith and Garbo to theater lobby displays. Unlike the Historical Records Survey, the bibliography was uniquely suited to Writers' Project requirements—to provide employment for needy but inexperienced people and at the same time to produce work impressive enough to convince Congress that it was more than a "boondoggle."

While some project people, demoralized by years of unemployment, spent their days in Third Avenue saloons, the thirty people assigned to the Motion Picture Bibliography—"M.P.Bib," in the project's argot—kept their noses to the grindstone. My first assignment took me to the 42nd Street library, but in a short time I was rewriting digests of films, alongside Phil and Lewis Morton, another supervisor.

Close to My Heart

No one could sample the mountain of information about movies without becoming both a fan and a film history buff. On weekends, Harold, Lewis, their wives-to-be, and Phil and I tracked down Russian films at the Cameo Theater on 7th Avenue or watched the latest French productions at art cinemas like the Little Carnegie on 57th Street. On Sunday nights, the six of us had supper at my parents' before walking to the Museum of Natural History, where the Museum of Modern Art's new Film Library was showing its first acquisitions. As news of the bibliography circulated (even *Variety* carried stories about it), old-timers in the industry—a cameraman who had worked for D. W. Griffith, an actor from Mack Sennett two-reelers—dropped by to reminisce. I read Terry Ramsaye's history of the movies, *A Thousand and One Nights*, in order to converse with them. Phil, a student of popular culture who had written articles on burlesque, vaudeville, and music for *New Masses* and *New Theatre*, also directed my attention to the social content of films and the industry's structure.

At his suggestion I went after work to the Labor Research Association, where Grace Hutchins and Anna Rochester gathered economic information for the labor movement. Gray-haired Grace Hutchins, a well-born New Englander who, like other New Women of the post–World War I generation, had devoted her life to social welfare, had moved steadily leftward until she and Rochester had joined the Communist Party. She introduced me to such basic research tools as *Reader's Guide to Periodical Literature,* the *New York Times Index,* and the *World Almanac,* as well as to the specialized Wall Street references that would enable me to investigate the film industry. After I dug out the stock holdings and interlocking directorships of the major film companies, Phil put the research together in an article, "Who Owns the Movies?" which appeared in *New Theatre* under the signature of Philip Sterling and Dorothy Dannen.

I can hardly overestimate my exhilaration during those months on the Writers' Project. I felt that I was allied to the forces of Good and that our side would prevail. I believed that communism was morally superior to capitalism, with its dog-eat-dog philosophy, and felt proud when the chairman of our shop unit said, "A Communist must be the best worker on the job." On May Day, 1936, I marched with thousands of actors, artists, and writers who carried placards reading "DEFEND THE ARTS PROJECT," "FREE THE SCOTTSBORO BOYS," and "HANDS OFF THE SOVIET UNION." When conservatives in Congress cut the appropriations for WPA, I drove a carload of people to Washington to parade in front of the Capitol and chant, "Give the bankers home relief. We want jobs." A fortnight later, funding for the Arts Projects was restored to the budget, thereby convincing me that if people joined together and raised their voices, they would win. It's still a political philosophy that I subscribe to.

Nineteen thirty-six was a remarkable year for the True Believer. Everyone seemed to be on our side. If you listened to the radio you would hear cowboy Gene Autry sing in praise of Mother Jones, who had been a hero in the coal fields, "The grand old champion of labor / known in every land." Another country singer made the Hit Parade with "Sixteen Tons": "You load sixteen tons and what do you get? / Another day older and deeper in debt."

At weekend cause parties a shy young man with a guitar sang, "I dreamed I saw Joe Hill last night, alive as you and me. / Says I, 'But Joe, you're ten years dead,' / 'I never died,' says he." The words were by poet Alfred Hayes, the music by guitarist Earl Robinson, making his first public appearances. He quickly outgrew the cause party circuit with his "Ballad for Americans," which Paul Robeson, then at the height of his popularity, turned into a hit. "Ballad" even became the theme song at the Republican National Convention in 1940.

If Earl Robinson was not at the party, Phil, who had a nice baritone, would go through his repertoire of Wobbly songs, from Joe Hill's "Pie in the Sky" and "The Rebel Girl" to the outrageous "There's Not a Crumb on the Bald Head of Jesus." When he sang

"Old Man River" and "Water Boy," I thought he sounded like Robeson.

Although we were still raising money for the Scottsboro boys, most of the parties I attended in the summer of 1936 were for the benefit of loyalist Spain. Spain's democratically elected government had been attacked by General Francisco Franco, with the backing of Hitler and Mussolini. The Soviet Union was helping the Loyalists, but the western democracies had declared a policy of neutrality. Save for the civil rights revolution more than two decades later, no cause ever seemed so right, so true, so urgent to support. During the next two and a half years, I attended meetings at Madison Square Garden, circulated petitions, marched in parades, collected money for the Spanish Loyalists.

Trade unionists, college students, Jewish kids from the Coops and husky longshoremen, Hollywood actors and screen writers—everyone seemed to be on our side. The Communist Party secretly recruited volunteer soldiers, including a youngster from the Motion Picture Bibliography, smuggling them across the Pyrenees to join the Abraham Lincoln Brigade. Only a small percentage of the volunteers were Party members, but the communists were taking the lead in "the good war" and I felt proud. There were mornings when I walked up the steps of the project building reciting to myself Wordsworth's words, written at the time of the French Revolution:

> Bliss was it in that dawn to be alive,
> But to be young was very heaven!

My emotional high was tempered when the press reported on the Moscow trials. A group of old Bolsheviks confessed that they had assassinated a member of the Soviet Politburo as part of a broad conspiracy to overthrow the government. During a second trial five months later, and a third in 1938, more men "admitted" that they had plotted with Germany, Japan, and Leon Trotsky to destroy the Soviet government.

Some communists and many who opposed the Party claimed that the trials were staged by Stalin and that the confessions had been elicited through torture or a "truth serum." I took the trials at face value, basing my belief not on the reports in the *Daily Worker* but on the authoritative *New York Times*. In the mid-30s, the *Times* was scarcely a left-wing paper. Opposed to FDR and the New Deal, it even employed several pro-fascist foreign correspondents. When Walter Duranty, the *Times* bureau chief in Moscow, wrote, "The confessions are true," I saw no reason to doubt him, especially when the correspondents for the Associated Press, United Press, and *Christian Science Monitor* came to the same conclusion, and U.S. Ambassador Joseph Davies wrote the president, "To have assumed that this proceeding was staged would be to presuppose the creative genius of a Shakespeare and the genius of a Belasco."

Two decades later we were horrified to learn that the Moscow trials had been only the tip of an iceberg diverting attention from Stalin's assassination of millions of Soviet citizens. Had this information been published in the *New York Times* in the 1930s, had Solzhenitsyn's exposé of the Soviet labor camps appeared then, would I have believed it? I am not sure. I was so full of admiration for the Soviet Union, the brave Spanish Loyalists, the feisty CIO, and so concerned by the threat of Hitler, that I might have written off reports of Stalin's "evil empire" as greatly exaggerated.

The Writers' Project was a daily battleground where Socialists, Troskyists, Lovestoneites, and Cannonites jeered at the Communists' blind loyalty to Moscow. Phil identified the splinter groups for me, pointing out 46-year-old James P. Cannon, a writer on the New York City guidebook, who had broken with the Party to start his own sect, and tall Philip Rahv who, with William Phillips, had edited the *Partisan Review* for the Communists but was now steering the magazine into the Trotskyist camp. Mary McCarthy, Rahv's wife at the time, reported that he signed in on the project each morning, then hurried home to work on the *Review*. When I puzzled over the animosity between socialists and communists, people who had grown up in the Coops sang a song that they had learned as YCLers:

> The cloakmakers union is a no good union.
> It's a company union by the boss.
> The Hillquits, Abe Cahans and Norman
>   Thomases*
> They make to the workers false promises.
> They preach socialism, but they practise
>   capitalism.
> What a loss!

This was followed by a new YPSL (Young People's Socialist League) ditty:

> Our line's been changed again.
> United fronts are what we love
> From below and from above.
> Our line's been changed again.
> The Party says the time has come
> Don't call a socialist a bum,
> Our line's been changed again.
> We must appear to be sedate,
> The Revolution
> it can wait

---

*Morris Hillquit, Abraham Cahan, and Norman Thomas were socialist leaders.

Our line's been changed again.

It was true. Frightened by fascism's growing strength, the Seventh Congress of the Communist International had decreed a United Front policy, a broad alliance of all parties on the left. Socialists and New Dealers were no longer to be characterized as "Social Fascists" but were to be wooed as allies in the struggle against Hitler and Mussolini. The American Communist Party shifted gears rapidly, muting criticism of FDR and the New Deal, and adopting as its slogan, "Communism Is Twentieth-Century Americanism." In addition to the writings of Marx and Lenin, International Publishers issued pamphlets containing the writings of Abraham Lincoln and Tom Paine; the Workers School was renamed the Jefferson School.

As the 1936 presidential campaign got under way, there was widespread concern that Roosevelt would be defeated by Republican Alfred Landon. A majority of the country's newspapers backed Landon; the *Literary Digest*, an influential weekly whose public opinion polls had hitherto been accurate, predicted his victory. Earl Browder was the Communist candidate, but Party leaders devised a pragmatic campaign tactic. When attempting to influence voters we were advised to say that of course Browder was our first choice but "if you can't vote for Browder, vote for Roosevelt." Roosevelt won by a landslide, and the *Literary Digest*, discredited by its error, went out of business.

Months before the election, Phil and I had decided to marry. The decision was not easily arrived at. I foresaw no difficulty in marrying someone who was "not our kind." His socialist background was romantic as well as politically correct. But Phil had qualms. Was he selling out the working class by marrying a girl from 79th Street who, despite her politics, retained middle-class values? Besides, there were his parents who would always be poor and needy. I pooh-poohed the obstacles and invited him home for dinner. Before accepting, he insisted on buying a new suit to replace his shiny frayed jacket and slacks.

So that is how it happened that Philip Sterling, looking handsome in a blue serge suit, purchased on time from Gimbels, had dinner with my parents. Not to ask for my hand—I would not have permitted such nonsense—but to give them a chance to talk with a prospective son-in-law. The dinner went reasonably well. Dad and Phil exchanged jokes, their one bond, while Mother hid her discomfort by ladling out enormous portions of meat and vegetables. After dinner we decided to go to the movies, thus giving Phil an opportunity to make a stand against bourgeois values. In the crowded apartment house elevator, every man whipped off his hat when he entered. Except Phil. Etiquette be damned. Down twelve floors, he kept his hat on and working-class honor intact. Mother blushed, Dad looked pained, and I tried not to laugh aloud.

The next day Mother called me to her bedroom for a tactful talk. She thought Phil very clever, but that incident in the elevator . . . Perhaps he didn't know any better. Surely I would inform him. As I anticipated, Mother's message had no effect. During the years that Phil visited my parents on 79th Street, he continued, like William Penn in the presence of King Charles, to keep his head covered in the elevator.

Mother and Dad were only a minor obstacle to our marriage. More of a problem was the government reg- ulation that forbade two family members from holding WPA jobs. Since the project began, there had been a good deal of pairing off, some couples living together while others married secretly to get around the regula- tion. Rejecting these alternatives, we agreed that one of us would have to get a job in what we then called private industry. Since I could claim secretarial skills, and there were more openings for secretaries than writers, I found a job first. In November 1936, I went to work on the *Architectural Forum*, a monthly magazine published by Time Inc.

6

The Time Inc. enterprises were housed in the Chrysler Building, whose art deco spire dominated the skyline of mid-Manhattan. Henry Luce had bought *The Forum* at the bottom of the depression because, he said: "To influence architecture is to influence life." A handsome spiral-bound magazine, its glossy pages covered new residential and industrial architecture. Although it earned a modest profit, it was never as successful as the other Time divisions: *Time*, *Fortune*, *March of Time*, and *Life* whose first issue, dated November 23, 1936 (my twenty-third birthday), appeared the week that I joined the company.

For $1.36 a week less than I had earned on WPA, I was a secretary to two young editors with whom I shared a narrow cubicle. I took dictation, typed letters and editorial copy and, on occasion, fetched coffee from the drugstore around the corner. Unlike the girls in the typing pool, who were graduates of business school, my secretarial skills were limited. George Nelson and Henry Wright tolerated sloppily typed letters and manuscripts, probably because I was a good listener and both had much to say.

Together they were the yin and yang of the magazine. Nelson, a graduate of Yale School of Architecture and a Prix de Rome scholar, brought me up to date on Le Corbusier, Mies van der Rohe, and the Bauhaus School, many of whose practitioners were now refugees from Hitler in the United States. In 1937, he was the first to import the bentwood furniture designed by Finnish architect Alvar Aalto. Henry Wright was the technical editor, specializing in environmental architecture. He was in charge of the magazine's Products and Practice section, which covered such new developments as radiant and solar heating. Occasionally he tossed me a manufacturer's press release and asked me to turn it into a news story for this section. This, of course, was strictly between us and did not alter my secretarial status.

In the Time Inc. hierarchy headed by publisher and managing editors, secretaries were close to the bottom of the totem pole. Only office boys were lower. Not all office boys, however. The majority of the boys who carried memos from floor to floor and placed copies of *Time* and *Life* on our desks each week were graduates of New York's high schools. But some were CBOBs — College Boy Office Boys who were graduates of Yale, Luce's alma mater, were often Somebody's Relative, and were being trained to move up rapidly in the company. In summer you could recognize them by their suntans, acquired during weekends on the family yacht. Some were diligent workers; others were careless and arrogant. Once I bawled out a CBOB who had lost photographs that George Nelson needed for a story. The following week he became a *Fortune* writer and cut me dead in the elevator. There were no CGOGs.

Although I had to grit my teeth and accept the CBOBs, they were only part of the culture shock I experienced during my first weeks on *The Forum*. Demographically, Time Inc. was poles away from WPA. The overwhelming majority of employees were upper-middle-class white Protestants (wasp; that handy acronym had not yet been invented). They were graduates of Yale, Princeton, Smith, and Bryn Mawr. Only a small number were Jews; there were no Negroes, not even in the mail room. In general, they were more competitive, more self-confident, and more affluent than Writers' Project staffers. They were also less radical. Executives were invariably Republicans, writers and researchers usually Democrats. But because this was still a time of economic and political crisis, there were enough disciples of Karl Marx on the magazines to make up a Communist Party unit to which I quickly transferred. The shop unit included people from each of the magazines plus a writer from the *New Yorker* or *Look*, where there were too few Reds to form a unit. We met at members' homes on Tuesday evenings, often opting for the Village apartment of a researcher with a powerful short-wave radio; at the end of a meeting we listened to English-language broadcasts from Spain.

My new comrades (we used the word affectionately) were serious Marxists. Each week we tackled Lenin on "Left-Wing Communism, an Infantile Disorder" or pamphlets by Marx and Engels. If someone raised questions about Russia's autocratic leader, others would remind us that the Soviet Union had not yet achieved the higher state of communism predicted by Marx and Lenin. Only after the emergence of Socialist Man, who put the welfare of the community above his own selfish interest, would the state wither away. This dream of Socialist Man working according to his abilities kept me a True Believer long after common sense should have dictated otherwise.

Marxist theory took up only part of each meeting. Shortly before my arrival, a group of *Fortune* editors, including Archibald Macleish, invited their *Forum* counterparts to lunch to propose that *Time* employees organize a chapter of the American Newspaper Guild, then beginning to hold negotiating sessions with several city newspapers. (The Newspaper Guild had a decided snob appeal. What writer was there who did not like to say, "I used to be a newspaperman myself"?) Affiliated with the CIO, the Guild was an industrial union, including typists as well as writers and researchers. When a sufficient number signed union cards we would ask Time management for a contract. Although the impetus for the union had come from *Fortune* writers, the communists quickly took the lead in recruiting. As soon as the news of the union reached management—and that was very soon; we were not clandestine—working conditions improved. Instead of the forty-four-hour week that brought us to the office on Saturday mornings, a forty-hour, five-day week was instituted. In addition, many received small raises; my salary went from $22.50 to $25 a week. If mere talk about a union brought these improvements, we pointed out to potential recruits, imagine how much better everyone would fare with a contract.

Union organizing took on the character of a crusade that year when nine million people were still jobless and the new sit-in movement was bringing companies like General Motors to the bargaining table. On Memorial Day, when striking workers and their families marched to the gates of the Republic Steel plant in Chicago, police and company guards shot them down. Pictures of the bloody battle, shown in newsreel theaters across the country, gave audiences a visceral shock, and assured new union members like me that we were part of a movement larger than ourselves, an idea whose time had come.

Talking union was not my only lunch-hour responsibility. At Party meetings we were asked to raise money for Spain, the *Daily Worker*, the Scottsboro boys. I don't know how the others managed, but I kept a mental list of fellow travelers with whom I lunched regularly. One was a college friend of Alice's who felt guilty because her family was wealthy; she always gave. Another, a Barnard classmate, brought me up short one day by saying, "You'll lose all your friends if you keep on asking for money." Soon afterward she shocked me further by joining our shop unit and doing her own collecting. Sometimes we worked with other progressives at Time. Instead of a party for Spain in a Greenwich Village walkup, we held a fundraiser in the posh town house of architect William Lescaze, with entertainment furnished by Leadbelly, a soon-to-be-chic black folksinger from the South.

Asking for money was unpleasant, but selling copies of the *Daily Worker*, as we were occasionally called on to do, was harder still. In an effort to broaden its audience, *Worker* editors brought out a Sunday edition, tabloid size, with stories and cartoons as well as political articles. To insure success for its first issue, every rank and file party member was expected to take to the streets with a bundle of papers. On the eve of publication half a dozen of us boarded the subway at 42nd Street and rode to Harlem, walking through the cars crying our wares in proper newsboy fashion. The sight of middle-class young people shouting "Get your *Sunday Worker*! Read all about it!" piqued the curiosity of subway riders. We sold most of our bundle, but I found the experience embarrassing and never repeated it. That first *Sunday Worker* should be a collector's item today, because it introduced B. Traven to the U.S. public with the first installment of his novel, *The Death Ship*. The issue also included a short story by Philip Sterling.

Although we did not make public announcements about our Communist Party membership, we were not very secretive, either. In the spring of 1938, when the company moved to the new Time & Life building on Rockefeller Plaza, *Architectural Forum* came up in the world. Henry Luce and his staff occupied the duplex penthouse suite on the south side of the thirty-third floor; *Architectural Forum*'s offices were on the north side. The drafting room and writers and researchers were located on the balcony, a flight of stairs away from the publisher and business staff. On slow days after an issue had gone to press we did an extraordinary amount of politicking there. Perhaps because we were physically separated from the eyes and ears of management, talk was uninhibited. One writer had a pamphlet by Lenin sticking out of his back pants pocket; others argued over a current *Daily Worker*, its pages spread open on a desk or drafting table. It's hard to believe now, but in the late 1930s—only a few doors upwind of Henry Luce—at least eight *Forum* staffers were members of the Communist Party. Along with people from *Time*, *Life*, and *Fortune*, the shop unit issued *High Time*, a neatly printed six-page paper which announced that it was "published by the Communist Party members at *Time.*" "Who then, are these Communists who are your fellow workers?" the initial editorial asked. "They are men and women who want a better world. The Communist Party desires and constantly works for a world in which there is no war, unemployment or poverty, a world in which there is that genuine democratic freedom that can come only through economic liberty."

The next issues, dated February and March 1939, contained articles pointing out the pro-Republican Party, anti-labor bias of *Time* and *Life*, the insecurity felt by Time, Inc. employees, and gossipy anecdotes about company executives. The third number of *High Time* was its last. Our line had changed again. In order to strengthen the democratic front against fascism the Party decided to dissolve "fractions"—that is, caucuses of Party members within unions. Thus papers like *High Time*, which set the communists apart from other union members, were abolished. *High Time* folded, but the decision to end caucuses in unions was quickly forgotten. Throughout my tenure at Time Inc., Party members regularly discussed union business and drew up slates of candidates for the annual elections.

Henry Luce wrote a memo calling the authors of *High Time* disloyal and subject to instant dismissal. The company even hired a detective to find out who was responsible for the publication. He could not have been very diligent; no action against us was ever taken. Red hunting was not yet fashionable in publishing circles. Time Inc. would have been criticized had it dismissed people for belonging to the Communist Party.

Phil and I married in May 1937, and after a three-day honeymoon settled into an apartment in Sunnyside, Queens, two stops on the El from Manhattan. Although our apartment lacked the charm of our friends' places in Greenwich Village, the rent was only $42.50 a month for three good-sized rooms. Fortunately, my parents believed that it was their duty to provide me with a trousseau, including everything from monogrammed towels and lace-trimmed underwear to furniture and table settings. Only once during the trousseau shopping did I put my foot down. Every bride in Mother's circle chose a silver pattern, from Tiffany if possible, but at least from Bloomingdales. Declaring that I was not going to waste my life polishing silver, I found a set of stainless steel flatware in Macy's Basement and returned the silver bowls and platters that we had received as gifts.

This was outlandish enough to set Mother's friends talking, but what really made our conventional apartment in the conventional borough of Queens unusual was the modern furniture that George Nelson designed for us. Planning to open his own design firm in the future (as he did in the 1940s), he was happy to have us to practice on, and we were delighted with the beautifully proportioned oak bedback, bureaus, and desk which we used for more than three decades.

Was there a conflict between our dream of world revolution and our pleasure in the simple lines and warm wood tones of our furniture? We certainly differed from the cartoon stereotype of the wild-eyed, baggy-trousered Bolsheviks, and so did everyone we knew. When we thought about it we answered doubts with the old saw, "Comes the Revolution, we'll all be eating strawberries and cream," or, as Phil liked to say, "Nothing is too good for the working class." After all, we were not living like the Rockefellers. Our windows rattled when an elevated train went by, and our neighbor's cockroaches soon found their way to our kitchen cupboard.

A real contradiction was the gulf between us and our neighbors, largely Catholic, blue-collar. The men went off to their jobs before we left in the morning; by the time Phil and I walked to the El the women were outside wheeling baby carriages. I could feel their stares, almost hear their comments as we turned the corner. I attributed their obvious dislike to anti-Semitism. No doubt that was a factor—there were no other Jews in the building—but the real sticking point was me. Not only did I have a job in Manhattan while they were housewives, but a year later, when we bought a second-hand car, I spent Saturday afternoons washing and polishing it. That was more than the women could bear. One of them was dispatched to tell me to "leave that for your husband. That's man's work." And then, "You'll make it hard for the rest of us."

The Party had no wisdom to offer for incidents like this. My response was to remain silent. In the three years that we lived there we never invited a neighbor to buy a raffle ticket for Loyalist Spain, to go to a Madison Square rally with us, or to visit our apartment.

Sure of his working-class loyalties—after all, his father was a house painter—Phil did not let the neighbors' animosity bother him. What did bother him in our first years of marriage was my cooking. Or rather my ignorance of cooking. In my last weeks at home I had asked Mother to give me a crash course, but when I couldn't work an eggbeater she said, as she had many times before and afterward, "You'll never learn." Alice was more helpful. She gave me *The Settlement House Cookbook*, the bible of all German-Jewish brides, with its subtitle *The Way to a Man's Heart*. I also bought the left-wing *Most for Your Money Cookbook* which, in the spirit of the 30s, told me how to stretch one's food budget with inexpensive meats (beef heart, cooking time four hours); this was interspersed with comments on the good things to be found in Moscow grocery stores. Neither book told me how to fry an egg or to cook meat. Phil, who could be endlessly patient when explaining a pamphlet by Lenin, was intolerant of fried eggs with broken yolks or undercooked chicken. When I served our first guests what he called "chicken with pink armpits," my reaction was that of the typical bride. I cried.

I shopped for dinner on my way home from work, and on Saturdays changed sheets and took the laundry to a store on Queens Boulevard. I washed the dishes, left money for the once-a-week cleaning woman, kept track of social engagements. I did all these things willingly and, except for cooking, with reasonable competence. Despite our advanced political beliefs, I was as responsible for household chores as my housewife neighbors were.

Never in the 1930s did I hear radicals discuss "the woman question." Communists looked on feminism as a middle-class movement, of little concern to the working class. Not until 1950 or so was "male chauvinism" discussed at Party meetings. The debate then was a tepid one, as was its conclusion: "Husbands should do the dishes." They didn't, or at least not in my household, until another two decades had gone by.

I wince as I read over what I have written. How could I have accepted the entire burden of housekeeping and, later, child care, without a murmur? In part because that was the way it was, the way it had always been. In part because we were not a stereotyped couple with a dominant male and subservient female. Phil was a frustrated writer who postponed his dream of writing the great American novel in order to hold routine jobs to support his family. Weekends and vacations were his time for plotting novels, writing short stories and, later, radio scripts. I could handle household chores more rapidly than he and was glad to give him the extra leisure for his writing. Equally important in avoiding a power struggle, I was better at arithmetic. Throughout our married life I took charge of paying the bills, balancing the checkbook, and deciding what to purchase with our income. In the 1930s and for decades afterward most wives had to ask their husbands for money; the reverse was true in our case.

During our first years of marriage, Congress continued to make drastic cuts in the Arts Projects. Phil had promised Harold Leonard that he would stay on WPA until the Motion Picture Bibliography was ready for the printer. To augment his income, he wrote articles for the *New York Times* entertainment section, sold a "Speaking of Pictures" on "Movie Kisses" to *Life,* and reviewed plays and films for the *Daily Worker.* The latter paid nothing but gave us free tickets to foreign films and for opening nights of such plays as Lillian Hellman's *The Little Foxes.*

These were exciting times for theater-goers. For 25 cents a ticket we saw WPA's all-black *Macbeth* and *Walk Together Chillun* in Harlem, and T. S. Eliot's

Murder in the Cathedral downtown. The latter was produced by John Houseman and his associate, 22-year-old Orson Welles. WPA also developed the Living Newspaper, a mixed-media documentary that combined actors, films, and shifting spotlights to tell of the plight of the American farmer in *Triple-A Plowed Under* and of the desperate need for housing in *One-Third of a Nation*. The set of the latter was a starkly realistic tenement house — members of the audience could almost smell the garbage — which went up in flames in the last act while a cast member shouted, "Can you hear me, Washington? Give me a decent home!"

Washington heard. The newly formed House Un-American Activities Committee summoned Hallie Flanagan, director of the Federal Theater, to testify, not only about the Living Newspaper but about such productions as *The Tragical History of Dr. Faustus* by Christopher Marlowe. "Who is this Marlowe? Is he a communist?" one Congressman asked. "Put it in the record that Marlowe was the greatest dramatist in the period immediately following Shakespeare," Mrs. Flanagan replied. People were vastly amused by the congressman's blunder, but he had the last laugh. The Project's appropriations were slashed, and the voice of the censor was soon loud and strong.

Welles and Houseman were rehearsing *The Cradle Will Rock*, a contemporary opera by composer Marc Blitzstein, who had been influenced by *The Threepenny*

Opera, the work of Kurt Weill and Bertold Brecht, anti-Nazi Germans. *Cradle*, a political satire about union organizing in Steeltown, U.S.A., featured Mr. Mister, the steel boss, his son Junior, and Larry Foreman, militant worker. The play had the vitality of *Waiting for Lefty* plus a rousing, singable score, but word reached Washington that it was "dangerous."

Phil and I had tickets for opening night. When we arrived at the Maxine Elliott Theater, a sign in the lobby said "NO SHOW TONIGHT." Sets, costumes, even the toupee worn by balding Howard Da Silva, who played Larry Foreman, were padlocked. Led by Da Silva and Will Geer, who played Mr. Mister, the would-be audience marched up 7th Avenue to the Venice Theater, on 58th Street. At 9:15 a faded curtain went up on a bare stage, with composer Blitzstein in his shirtsleeves seated at an old upright piano. Actors Equity and the Musicians Union had forbidden their members to appear on stage in the unauthorized performance, but when Blitzstein played the opening number, one voice, than another and another, joined him from the orchestra pit and balcony. Before the play was over, cast members were dancing and singing in the center aisle where Larry Foreman confronted Mr. Mister. It was almost midnight when the enthusiastic audience filed out of the theater, singing the play's catchy tunes. The next morning New York's newspapers reviewed the "runaway opera" on their front pages, generally agreeing that it was "an exciting savagely humorous social cartoon" and "the most exciting propagandistic tour de force" since *Waiting for Lefty. Cradle Will Rock* became the first production of Welles's and Houseman's Mercury Theater, but the Federal Theater Project was nearing its end.

One of Phil's rare paid jobs then was the promotion of *Blockade*, a Hollywood film that supported Loyalist Spain. Calling the conflict "not war but murder," the picture ended with an appeal to the "conscience of the world." Phil worked nights and weekends sending out a stream of publicity stories and arranging benefit performances of left and liberal audiences. But neither *Blockade* nor *The Spanish Earth*, the documentary financed by such writers as Ernest Hemingway, Dorothy Parker, and Archibald Macleish—even Henry Luce contributed—could save the embattled republic. With overwhelming military force on their side, Franco's armies took Barcelona and laid siege to Madrid.

On a blustery night in March 1939, Phil and I were in Times Square with Curt Reiss and his friend Rudolph Breda, recently returned from California, where he had helped found the Hollywood Anti-Nazi League, a major fundraising organization for the Loyalists and the German underground. We had come to the Square because the band of electric lights moving around the *Times* building spelled out the news before it could be heard on the radio. Madrid had fallen; Franco's forces were pouring into the city. I shall never forget Breda's stricken countenance. We talked romantically about the revolution, but he was the real thing, a man who had escaped from Germany and was a driving force of the anti-fascist movement in Europe and the United States. Phil and I guessed that he was a Comintern agent; so, probably, did Lillian Hellman; she used him as the model for her anti-fascist hero (played by Paul Lukas) in *Watch on the Rhine*. Decades later I read that Rudolph Breda had been a pseudonym for Willi Munzenberg, German publisher and Reichstag deputy who, after fleeing the Third Reich, had organized anti-fascist councils in London, Paris, and New York. Less than a year and a half after our meeting in Times Square he was found hanging from a tree on a road in France, presumably killed by Soviet agents after he had broken with the Comintern.

Our car, a Studebaker roadster with red leather upholstery and a rumble seat, purchased for $200, enabled us to escape work and politics on occasional weekends. We toured the Pine Barrens of New Jersey and drove to Jasper Deeter's Hedgerow Theatre in Pennsylvania, an early regional playhouse. The roads were lined with hitchhikers, and we never failed to pick up someone interesting. Once, it was an African prince who was attending college in the United States to prepare himself for leadership when he returned home. Another time, a teenager who worked for the Civilian Conservation Corps brought us to his camp for lunch. We ate in a big barracks, enjoying the franks and beans and the healthy youngsters, most of them city boys who were having their first experience working outdoors. We also managed a week's vacation on Cape Cod where Frank Shay, now retired from WPA, found us a cabin in the woods in Wellfleet. We spent our days on the Great Beach — so empty that we could go skinny-dipping — and walking the sand flats of the bay at low tide, gathering oysters and quahogs.

My rather boring days on *The Forum* were enlivened when the magazine published special issues. For an issue on Frank Lloyd Wright, the great man himself climbed the stairs to the balcony, giving me a chance to admire his flowing white hair, flamboyant cape, and enormous ego. The best of the special issues as far as I was concerned was the one on the World's Fair, published in June 1939. The fair, whose theme was "The World of Tomorrow," was located in Flushing Meadow, only a few El stops from our apartment. Armed with passes from *The Forum*, one of my job's few perks, we spent many Saturdays and Sundays there.

With the fascist countries unrepresented, the fair promised a world of peace and prosperity. The General Motors Futurama showed streamlined cars, and homes with glass brick and plywood interiors and such mechanical marvels as washing machines and dishwashers. An exhibit in the Medicine and Public Health building was called "The Retreat of Death." The Scandinavian pavilions were models of good design; the Swiss and Danish restaurants offered continental food at prices we could afford.

The Soviet Pavilion, voted the most popular in a Gallup poll, was a monumental building topped by a giant figure of a worker holding aloft a red star. Aesthetically I preferred the sculpture of Carl Milles and Paul Manship, on view elsewhere, but the Soviet exhibits were impressive: a full-scale reproduction of a Moscow subway station, startlingly clean by U.S. standards, and photographic murals of great dams and collective farms. Affable women guides answered even hostile questions patiently and distributed copies, bound in imitation leather, of the new Soviet Constitution, which guaranteed civil liberties for all citizens. The future as we saw it included gleaming new machines, cure-all medicines, handsome furniture, good food—and socialism.

The world of tomorrow was very much on my mind in the summer of 1939. I was almost 26 years old, and the girls I had gone to school and camp with already had one or two children. Shouldn't Phil and I start a family? I felt no sudden maternal urge, had never even held a baby in my arms, but my conventional self was saying, *it's time*. Less conventionally, I never considered quitting work to become a full-time mother. We could manage a baby on two incomes if I was guaranteed my job back after the child was born.

For this I turned to the Newspaper Guild, which was negotiating its first contract with Time Inc. Sessions were held after work, and I attended as an observer. Henry Luce was chief negotiator for the company until his stiff missionary's son manner gave way before the slangy street smarts of Milton Kaufman, spokesman for the Guild. One evening when Luce made a particularly stuffy comment, Kaufman countered with, "Nuts, Mr. Luce." "I do not understand your language," Luce frostily replied. "Nuts, Mr. Luce, you know what I mean," Kaufman said. At the next bargaining session, Henry Luce was replaced by his younger brother Sheldon.

Months of negotiations brought the two sides together on wages, hours, vacation pay. Time Inc. prided itself on being a generous employer, and the conditions were as good as or better than in other city contracts. When on an August evening they discussed maternity leave, Sheldon Luce said, "We want our employees to have babies." The company agreed to a six-month maternity leave with double vacation pay and a guarantee of rehiring—a better clause than today's Family and Medical Leave Act offers. I went home in triumph to report the news. By late September I was pregnant. The day that I paid my first visit to an obstetrician, Phil lost his WPA job.

7

The fall of 1939 ushered in a difficult period for True Believers. On August 22, Hitler and Stalin signed a non-aggression pact. It was shocking to see photographs of the Nazi foreign minister being feted in Moscow and to read that Stalin had proposed a toast to Hitler. So abrupt was the Soviet shift of position that the Sunnyside branch of the Communist Party sent a well-briefed comrade to every Party household in the neighborhood to explain its significance. Even before he rang our doorbell, Phil and I had concluded that the pact was a triumph of diplomacy on Stalin's part. Hadn't England and France excluded the Soviet Union from the Munich talks that gave Hitler a free hand in Czechoslovakia? Hadn't the western democracies repeatedly rejected an alliance with the Russians? The West had been signaling Hitler to move eastward. Now Stalin had cleverly turned the tables, buying time to strengthen his country's defenses.

We were so comfortable with this line of reasoning that we went ahead with plans for a week's vacation on Cape Cod. We were having breakfast in a luncheonette in Wellfleet when we heard the first radio report of Hitler's invasion of Poland. Two days later Great Britain and France declared war against Germany, marking the beginning of World War II. When the Soviet Union marched into Poland soon afterward, we believed that the Red Army came as liberators, to free the Poles from an oppressive regime. "Why doesn't Stalin march into my country, too?" Frances Jezek asked. That winter, American communists walked a fine ideological tightrope as they continued to justify the Soviet alliance with Hitler. The American League Against War and Fascism, hitherto a militant anti-Nazi organization, changed its name to the American League for Peace and Democracy, and then the American Peace Mobilization; the Hollywood Anti-Nazi League was renamed the Hollywood League for Democratic Action. We were only slightly disturbed when the Russians invaded Finland in late November. After all, the Finnish border was twenty miles from Leningrad, and Stalin's demand for a buffer zone seemed reasonable; besides, the Finnish government was notoriously reactionary, with close ties to the Nazis. It was not until April, when Hitler's forces occupied Norway, blitzkrieged their way through the Low Countries, and marched into France, that the character of the war seemed to change.

I had many things to preoccupy me during those months. When Phil received his pink slip from WPA in

September, the unemployment rate was 17 percent and the likelihood of a job slim. He still spent part of each day helping Harold Leonard complete the first volume of the Motion Picture Bibliography; *The Film as Art* was published by the Museum of Modern Art Film Library in 1941. The remaining files were stored at the museum until 1985, when *The Film in Society* and *The Film as Industry* were finally published, with an introduction by Philip Sterling, the only surviving editor. To his surprise, Phil found work almost immediately when the owner of a chain of art cinemas hired him to manage the Pelham Playhouse in Westchester County. As manager he had to oversee every detail, from the lights on the marquee to supplying the cashier with proper change at the beginning of the theater day and locking away the receipts in the office safe at its end. Because he lacked time to commute from Sunnyside, he rented a room in Pelham, and I joined him on weekends.

By then an obstetrician—a comrade obstetrician, of course—had confirmed my pregnancy. Since we would need a larger place when the baby was born, I began to look at apartments in Pelham. I found big, sunny apartments with tree-covered yards where, because of the Depression, rents were as low as in Sunnyside and owners offered paint jobs and big refrigerators. After I had seen two or three places that I was enthusiastic about, I made a date to have the real estate agent show them to Phil.

As we got into his car the following Saturday, the realtor put one foot on the running board, then asked, "Mr. Sterling, are you Jewish?" To Phil's "yes" he said, "I'm sorry, but no apartment house in Pelham will rent to Jews."

Wordlessly we scrambled out of the car and returned to the theater lobby. We had heard of restrictive covenants but never thought that they would apply to us. When friends came by to take us to lunch, they were indignant. "You ought to report this to the Anti-Defamation League," one suggested. At just that moment, Phil's boss came out of his office to ask what had happened. He left without commenting, but five minutes later he called Phil in and fired him. Jewish himself, he feared that a protest by Phil could result in a boycott of the theater as well as another he owned in nearby Mount Vernon.

At the end of the show that night Phil collected his final paycheck and we drove back to New York. Sunnyside with its crowded streets and noisy El had never looked better. Even though it was many months before Phil found another job, Pelham's snub did not continue to rankle. It merely confirmed what we knew: that things were wrong with the world and we must continue to work to change them. Phil wrote articles for *Film*, a scholarly quarterly, for the weekly *Hollywood Reporter*, for the *Times* and *Daily Worker*. He finally went to work for Nu-Art Films, distributors of 16-

millimeter films to schools and other non-theatrical outlets. The work was routine, but the salary of $40 a week seemed munificent.

I continued to grow large in appropriate places and to become heartily sick of my two navy blue maternity dresses. (Navy blue was the only available color then; pregnant women were supposed to look inconspicuous.) I had fudged the baby's anticipated arrival date so that I worked until the end of my seventh month of pregnancy and thus would have four months at home with the baby. By the time I left *The Forum*, top heavy but pleased with myself, we had rented a house in Sunnyside Gardens, a pioneer garden apartment development that had been designed by *Forum* editor Henry Wright's father. On a tree-lined street only a few blocks from our old apartment, one and two-family houses were grouped around a common court, which was planted with grass and shrubs. It was the first time I had lived in a house: three small bedrooms upstairs, living room, dining room, and kitchen on the main floor, and a basement with furnace and laundry tub. Best of all was the tiny backyard, where a mountain ash tree grew and I hoped to plant flowers. Rent: $56 a month, plus coal for heating and hot water.

With two months to spare before the baby's birth — the only free time I would have for decades — I tried to educate myself about baby and child care. There were no maternity courses for new mothers, and Dr. Spock was a young pediatrician in New York. In Time Inc's Morgue and the local library I found a few books about the birth process but little about child behavior. Since none of my friends had children, Mother was my only authority. While I put little faith in her knowledge of child psychology, I gratefully accepted her expertise on layettes. Together we went to Macy's to select a bewildering array of tiny shirts and wrappers. Our purchases were not to be shipped until Mother phoned the salesgirl to report on the sex of the baby. Otherwise the store would not know whether the garments were to be trimmed with pink or blue.

Only when we were shown the latest in aluminum sterilizers did I speak up. "That won't be needed," I said, "because I'm going to nurse the baby." Breastfeeding, I soon discovered, was old-fashioned, almost indecent. The modern way to feed infants was to prepare a formula of canned milk, water, and dextrose, to be dispensed from a sterilized bottle. I was determined to nurse the baby, on the same romantic principle that I was having one — to experience life at its fullest. Mother and her friends, the salesclerk, and even my obstetrician disapproved. It was he who asked the question that soon became familiar: "Do you want to be like a cow?"

During the same visit he cheerily informed me that I had a fifty-fifty chance of having a boy. Since almost everyone preferred boys, this was a standard ob/gyn joke, to keep the patient happy. He also told me that he delivered babies at Brooklyn Jewish Hospital or at Beth Israel in Manhattan. I gulped. Both hospitals would sound too Jewish to my parents, whose social circle patronized Mt. Sinai Hospital (German-Jewish) or non-sectarian hospitals like Lenox Hill. But how could I bring this up without sounding anti-Semitic? My father knew. "Do you want to eat kosher food for two weeks?" he asked. When neither Phil nor the obstetrician put forward a counterargument, the doctor arranged for me to go to LeRoy Sanitarium, a small private hospital.

The last days of May and June dragged. The *New York Times*, left on our doorstep every morning, brought news of the Nazi conquest of France — German soldiers goosestepping down the Champs-Elyséees — and the evacuation of British troops from Dunkirk. I, self-absorbed, donned a smock and a pair of Phil's pants and tackled the backyard. The grass I planted never survived, but some morning glory vines grew around the back steps. I was tying them to the uprights of our little porch when I felt my first labor pains.

Mother obligingly fetched me and my overnight bag and drove me to LeRoy. By evening there was quite a gathering in my hospital room — Mother and Dad, Phil and Alice, and at long last the doctor. He gave me an anaesthetic to ease the pain — no one worried about its effect on the baby—and as I drifted in and out of consciousness the others listened to a radio broadcast from the Republican National Convention. Shortly after midnight on June 28, Wendell Willkie was nominated for president, and I heard the doctor say, "It's a boy."

The next day Phil and I put several names in a hat and picked out Peter. That the names we chose from were all common Christian ones never occurred to us. After all, when Phil wrote for the *Daily Worker* he signed reviews "Peter Sidney."

In 1940 new mothers—middle-class ones, anyway—stayed in bed for two weeks. My radical doctor prescribed a ten-day hospital stay, ordering me to dangle my legs over the side of the bed on the first post-natal day, put my feet on the floor on day two, and walk down the corridor thereafter. While Mother's friends predicted dire effects on my innards and a nurse followed me down the hall lest I fall, I obeyed the doctor. I learned only later that LeRoy's was a place where wealthy women went for abortions or alcoholism cures. The hospital had no resident doctor, so if anything had gone wrong with Peter or me we would have been in trouble. But what could go wrong? My private room, paid for by Blue Cross, was large and bright. White-coated waiters brought in meals, whisking silver domes off dishes to show me Eggs Benedict, poached salmon, sweetbreads, and other unaccustomed delicacies. Books were stacked on my bedside table and my reading was interrupted only when a nurse brought in Peter for a feeding.

Despite my belief that breastfeeding was a natural and pleasurable process, Peter had a frustrating time nursing, and my nipples were soon cracked and sore. I was bucking both the current squeamishness about women's bodies and the propaganda of the manufacturers of infant formula, who flooded the medical profession with studies "proving" that bottle feeding was the modern, scientific way. In the 1930s and 1940s only one woman in four nursed her baby. At LeRoy's, breastfeeding disrupted normal routine. The nurses gave Peter bottles at night, thereby diminishing his need for my milk. By the time we returned home I was running a high fever. The obstetrician diagnosed caked milk, gave me X-ray treatments to clear it up, and prescribed a canned milk formula for Peter. The sterilizer from Macy's was put to good use.

Except for this setback, the first months of Peter's life went smoothly. A pleasant baby nurse, paid for by my parents, spent three weeks teaching me how to care for him. The first time I bathed him I inadvertently ducked his head underwater. As he came up sputtering, Mother said her familiar "You'll never learn." But I did. By the time the nurse left I felt comfortable handling the tiny creature, who grew larger and more responsive every day. Fortunately, he was a "good" baby who soon slept through the night and smiled winningly.

When he cried, which wasn't often, I picked him up or rocked him in his carriage, no-nos with child care experts who feared "spoiling" the baby and advised rigid schedules. From the young mothers who gathered in backyards on sunny days, I learned of a new theory of child care, influenced by Freud and his disciples, which opposed thwarting the child and advocated feeding on demand. My need for an organized day was too great for demand feeding, but Peter accepted a schedule which called for his first bottle and pureed banana around 8:00 A.M. and his last at 8:00 P.M., thus preparing him for my return to work.

The Sunnyside mothers were shocked to learn that I planned to work when Peter was four months old. In answer to questions that were almost hostile, I defended myself by saying that I worked because we needed the income. This was not entirely true. Much as I loved my son, I was bored with plotting his weight gains on a graph and trying new brands of baby food. I was eager to return to the magazine, to talking politics and recruiting members for the union.

There were no day care centers for working mothers, and no one I knew even employed a nanny or au pair girl, but with unemployment still high the Urban League office in Harlem could supply a domestic worker to take care of Peter, cook and clean, and sleep in the tiny bedroom next to ours. After several unsuccessful tries, we were lucky to find Annette Smith Lee, a black woman of fine intelligence and humor who captivated Peter immediately.

In addition to caring lovingly for Peter, Annette was a superb cook. Trained to work for wealthy people, she served us gourmet dinners. Her Yorkshire pudding was a triumph, her apple pie perfection, and she could even make broccoli palatable. With these qualifications, why was she working as a live-in domestic for a salary of $125 to $150 a month? (The salary may sound shockingly low, but at that time it represented almost all of my monthly earnings.) It was a year or two before she trusted us enough to tell us about her last job. Employed by a wealthy family on Long Island, she was serving breakfast to her boss one morning when he complained that his coffee was cold. "What kind of breakfast is this to serve to a white man?" he asked. Annette returned to the kitchen for the coffee pot, poured its contents over his head, packed her bags, and left. She was too full of anger, she realized, to work for people who treated her as an inferior.

Noting my youth and inexperience when she first came to Sunnyside for an interview, she decided that ours was a household where she could take charge. To establish herself as a figure of authority she gave her age as ten years older than she was. She further made herself indispensable by cooking our weekend meals before she left on Saturdays so that I promptly forgot the little cooking I had learned. Her presence was my first encounter with a black woman, hers with white people who respected her. I felt no qualms about becoming an employer. We paid the going wage, were scrupulously fair about hours and overtime, and were soon able to breach her defenses and become friends — a friendship that lasted until her death almost three decades later. While we saw eye to eye on child care, her cooking kept me in thrall, just as she hoped it would. Ten years later, when the time came for us to part, I postponed the decision for months because I was terrified at the thought of starting to cook again. I still dream of Annette's apple pie.

Although I missed Peter, it was good to be back at work exchanging ideas with *Forum* staffers and union members at lunch. Politics was a touchy subject on the north balcony in the winter of 1940–41, when waves of Nazi bombers were pounding Britain, leaving thousands homeless or dead. Almost everyone listened to Ed Murrow's nightly broadcasts, introduced by his staccato "London Calling!", but when a member of the art department solicited contributions for Bundles for Britain, the True Believers turned her down. Both Great Britain and Germany were imperialist powers, we said, and our goal was to keep the United States out of the war. We had strange bedfellows, not only the Socialists and Trotskyists but the right-wing America

Firsters, many of them with Nazi ties. As I looked at *Life's* photographs of bombed-out London, I found it difficult to believe that there was no difference between Great Britain and Germany. Nevertheless, I hewed to the Party line, even when it led me to do something I was quickly ashamed of. For five years we had boycotted German goods. After the Nazi-Soviet pact, the Party called off the boycott and I bought a pair of German-made poultry shears on sale at the local hardware store. They were well-constructed shears—German steel products were the best in the world at that time—but I soon stopped using them because they came to symbolize both Nazi brutality and my failure to think for myself. I still have the shears. Every once in a while I bring them out and deliver a short lecture on intellectual honesty.

Peter learned to crawl, then to walk; he scrambled up the stairs and scooted down again. He was practicing his accomplishment in the back yard on a Sunday in June, the week before his first birthday, when our next door neighbor slammed back her screen door and shouted, "Germany has invaded the Soviet Union." On porch after porch people brought out radios to hear the news. Not every householder in Sunnyside Gardens was a member of the Communist Party, but those who were shared the same emotions—horror at the slaughter that was to come, and a feeling of relief. After twenty-two months we were back in the mainstream. Peace organizations were disbanded and we helped to organize Russian War Relief.

Following the invasion, Phil changed jobs. Artkino, the Soviet agency in charge of film distribution in the United States, had an office in the same 7th Avenue building that housed Nu-Art Films. Before the Nazi attack, Artkino had barely been able to attract audiences to the dingy Cameo Theater on 41st Street. Afterward, as a wave of sympathy for the Russians swept the country, their films opened with fanfare on Broadway. Phil gladly relinquished writing blurbs for Laurel and Hardy two-reelers in favor of publicizing such films as Eisenstein's *Alexander Nevsky* and *One Day in the Soviet Union*. When the Russians began to drive back the German army, American sympathy was translated into lend-lease shipments of food and war matériel and Phil felt with considerable justice that he was playing a tiny part in stopping the Nazi juggernaut. He worked 10-hour days, 6-day weeks, and gave up vacations to arrange screenings for film critics, to rewrite the films' wooden English subtitles, even to translate the words of the "Song of the Soviet Tankmen" when Fred Waring and his Pennsylvanians recorded it.

Before hiring him, Artkino's American chief bluntly told him that if he was a member of the Communist Party he must immediately resign. Tass, the Soviet news agency, and Amtorg, its trading company, maintained the same policy for U.S. employees. If there were Russian spies in the United States, I felt sure that they were not working through the American Communist Party; it would be another half century before I learned differently. Meanwhile, from the summer of 1941 until the end of the war, Phil avoided Party meetings; we even canceled our subscription to the *Daily Worker*.

My job changed, too. *The Architectural Forum* had never lived up to Henry Luce's expectations as a moneymaker. When staff cuts were decreed, I was among the expendable. Fortunately, Time had a benevolent employment policy, which permitted me, the week before the Japanese attack on Pearl Harbor, to shift to *Life*, at first as a secretary and then as a researcher.

Life, with its striking photographs and big format—spread open it was larger than my television screen is today—was the most influential magazine in the country during the war. Millions turned to it each week for the latest pictures from the battlefront. Like other Time magazines it was produced by a hierarchy of editors and department heads, but the basic working structure was the researcher-writer team. Researcher was a category invented by *Time*. All researchers were women, all writers men. *He* came up with the idea for a story. *She* investigated it and drew up a list of picture possibilities. *He* okayed her picture script and arranged to have a photographer assigned to the story. *She* accompanied the photographer and took notes for picture captions. After *she* turned over her research to the writer, *he* wrote the story. Throughout this process the researcher was on call, ready to supply additional facts. To signify gaps in his information that the writer wished her to fill in, he interspersed the word "Koming": "John Smith, Koming years old," "Mary Jones, Koming-eyed housewife." The record for these interpolations was held by a writer whose article had sixty Komings, his prize sentence reading "In Koming, Chiang Kai-Shek met with Koming and they declared Koming."

When the story was completed, the researcher checked it for accuracy. She read carefully, putting a pencil dot over each word to indicate that it was correct. Proper names and dates were verified by a red-pencil dot, signifying that they had been confirmed by an unimpeachable source. (The *New York Times* and other daily papers were not considered red checks.) If her writer said "Cyrus Ching, looking like one of Disney's seven dwarfs," she examined a picture of the dwarfs, comparing them with a photograph of Ching. If writer and researcher disagreed on which Disney character Ching resembled, he composed another simile. Or if he insisted on his fanciful phrase, he said, "I'll initial it," meaning that he would take responsibility for the sentence's accuracy. Otherwise the researcher was blamed for all errors.

The work had something of the challenge of a crossword puzzle. On any given day I might have to find out the color of the eyes of the Speaker of the House, the height of the Washington Cathedral, the number of seats in the Metropolitan Opera House. The one thing no researcher ever said was "I can't find out." Time Inc. helped with a well-run morgue containing books and clippings, and a doctor, lawyer, and historian were available to answer questions. Besides, there were other sources in New York—ad agencies, museum staffs, press agents—all eager to please *Life*. For out-of-town stories Time had its domestic and foreign news bureaus, where staff people or free-lancers replied quickly to telephone calls and wires.

On one of my first assignments I spent a day in the library of the Museum of Natural History compiling five fact-filled pages on frogs so my writer could caption a striking photograph of a spring peeper in full voice. Later I spent a month touring the Waldorf Astoria Hotel from roof to sub-basement, cataloguing its picture possibilities, which ranged from a chef's culinary masterpiece to a storage bin heaped high with soap and toilet paper. Then, picture script in hand, I accompanied Alfred Eisenstadt when he shot an essay on the hostelry.

The researchers' grapevine kept us informed on which writers were pleasant to work for, which unnerving. The National and Foreign News Departments worked on a Tuesday–Saturday week in order to cover late-breaking news. Back-of-the-book stories—on nature, art, science—were completed in a more leisurely fashion from Monday to Friday. I tried to avoid Foreign News editor David Cort, who not only said that he could tell a communist by looking into her eyes but whose stories invariably closed after midnight Saturday because he had a multi-cocktailed dinner before turning in his copy. Nor did I like to work for tall, languid Noel Busch, who came in at noon and was the only writer with a couch in his office. A privileged character because he had worked with Luce from *Time*'s early days, he was so impressed with his own importance that I found him overbearing. Russell Davenport, who had been Wendell Willkie's leading advocate, wrote *Life*'s editorials. Occasionally when his researcher was away I had to fill in for her. Davenport was pleasant enough, but he voiced such Big Thoughts that I had difficulty understanding him.

Most of the time "my" writer was Joseph Kastner, an amiable redhead, active in the Newspaper Guild, who never pulled rank and who roamed the back-of-the-book doing features on ballet and opera, aviation and nature. I interviewed ballerinas, held lights for Eisenstadt when he photographed the Metropolitan Opera House for a glittering two-page spread, and boned up on aviation for text pieces on the business and poetry of flying.

Most of the photographers were young and pleasant to work with. Occasionally one made a pass at a researcher, but there was little of what today would be called sexual harassment. A researcher's main problem came when she was assigned to work with topflight people like Margaret Bourke White or Alfred Eisenstadt. I never worked with Bourke White because she was usually overseas, but I did several stories with Eisenstadt, a German refugee who began using a Leica when the rest of us were in kindergarten. A good thing about teaming up with Eisy was that his stories "made the book," while many others never saw publication. But most researchers found him arrogant and self-preoccupied.

For me the nature stories were best of all. In the 1940s, the country's leading nature photographers, men like Roger Tory Peterson, Eliot Porter, Ansel Adams, and Rutherford Platt, submitted their pictures to *Life*. I gave myself a quick course on avian behavior and brushed up on botany to supply my writer with interesting facts on baby birds, insectivorous plants, winter buds, and autumn colors. Besides the joy of learning, there were perks—extra photographs of fledgling birds, snakes, and frogs to take home to Peter as well as tickets to the opera and ballet.

The work was so pleasant that I seldom wondered why only men could write. Later in the war, when many writers were drafted, there were occasional exceptions to this rule. The fashion editor—she could be distinguished from the rest of us because she wore her hat in the office—sometimes wrote her own stories, but they were gone over carefully by one of the men. Occasionally a woman with aspirations as a writer quit in disgust, but most of us accepted the writer-researcher division without questioning it. Not only accepted it but were brainwashed into believing that it was inevitable. Once when Joe Kastner was overworked he handed me a Letters column and asked me to write the short editorial comment that followed each letter. I sat there with a blank piece of paper in my typewriter, unable to put down a word; after an hour Joe laughed and took the pages away.

Most days passed so quickly that it was not until 5:00 P.M. that I was suddenly filled with foreboding. Suppose something had happened to Peter? Why hadn't I called home? I rode the bus impatiently, willing it to hurry when late afternoon traffic slowed it down, then jogged the three cross-town streets to our house. During the long summer days, Peter waited for me outside; in winter he was in the living room, where he submitted to a brief hug before inspecting the contents of my briefcase. In addition to fat red Time Inc. copy pencils and paper to scribble on, he might discover a toy I had bought in the 5 and 10 during lunch hour or photographs from stories I was working on.

At dinner he sat in his high chair, joining in if not dominating the conversation. Our art moderne table had a tubular metal frame — contemporary-looking but wobbly — and overturned glasses of milk were a daily occurrence. After our not-so-gracious dinner I bathed Peter and read from one of the many books he was acquiring. On Saturdays I pushed him in his stroller to the public library to stock up on books for the week ahead. Mother Goose and Grimm fairy tales had their place, but I also steered him to realistic books like *Mike Mulligan and His Steam Shovel*, *Little Toot*, the story of a tugboat, and a series on cave, cliff, and tree dwellers that Phil recalled from his Socialist Sunday school days. At four, Peter was sufficiently well versed in the theory of evolution to explain it to his friend Dennis Murphy, two doors away. His explanation must have been clear because the next day Dennis's mother forbade him to play with Peter.

The trip to the library was only one of many Saturday excursions. Peter was the first kid on the block to tour the neighborhood firehouse and railroad switching yards. By the time he was three we went to the Museum of Natural History to see the dioramas of Native American and African life that fascinated me as a child. At four I judged him ready for the Museum of Modern Art and the ballet, where we had orchestra seats courtesy of *Life*. The walls of his room were decorated with reproductions of paintings by Picasso,

Renoir, and Miró, which I hoped would shape his taste in art. The record player in the living room introduced him to Paul Robeson singing "Ballad for Americans" and songs from the Spanish Civil War. Later a Young People's Record Club shipped monthly selections: songs from the American Revolution, folk and union songs recorded by Pete Seeger and the Almanac Singers. Red diaper babies started their education early.

Phil was too busy at Artkino to join us in our expeditions, but he was as concerned as I with Peter's development. We had read that Russian child care experts trained children, from infancy onward, to become members of a socialist society. In a book on Soviet nursery schools, I found pictures of three-person play pens in which toddlers learned to share toys and play together. Putting a second child into Peter's one-person pen resulted in toy-snatching and tears, but another photograph in the book looked practical. Instead of the traditional rectangular jungle gym that children climbed alone, this was tent-shaped, so that two youngsters using it at the same time would end up face-to-face when they reached the top. A local carpenter easily replicated it, and the jungle gym was used in our yard for a decade, then passed along to friends. Whether it moved the climbers a rung closer toward Socialist Man, I cannot say.

The efforts I put into Peter's upbringing were motivated in part by guilt at being away from him, guilt caused to a considerable extent by the mothers who stayed home. "Poor little Peter," a neighbor said. "He just stands outside waiting for you to come home." "How can you bear to leave your child in the hands of a stranger?" another asked. Nor did the teachers at the Sunnyside Progressive Nursery School do anything to reassure me. Once when I protested at the number of school holidays in February—two presidential birthdays and Valentine's Day!—the head teacher loftily proclaimed, "We don't believe in working mothers."

The feelings of foreboding that assailed me at the end of the day were heightened after the United States entered the war. In the first weeks after Pearl Harbor an air raid alarm warned that German planes were approaching New York; there were also rumors of Nazi submarine landings on Long Island. Some days it seemed unbearable to remain in Manhattan, leaving Peter in Queens, perhaps in the pathway of a bomb. With the organization of a civilian defense system these fears lessened. New York was blacked out at night; theater marquees and advertising signs were turned off and every home was equipped with black-out curtains. After dark, air raid wardens patrolled the streets, knocking on doors if a pencil-thick beam of light showed through a window. Becoming a small cog in the warning system, I sat at a telephone switchboard in Long Island City two nights a week, prepared to spread the alarm if enemy planes were sighted. None ever appeared, but I still have a blue card identifying me as a Citizens' Defense Worker.

Mother joined the American Women's Volunteer Corps, received training in first aid, and was certified as a driver in case of emergency. Proud of her well-tailored grey uniform, she came to show it to us one Saturday when Phil's mother was visiting. The grandmothers made polite conversation at lunch, trying to get along despite the considerable differences in their backgrounds until Peter, squirming in his high chair, knocked a cup of hot coffee over himself. When he screamed, both women went into action. Using the tried and true cure for burns, Phil's mother smeared his reddened hands with margarine. My mother, who had learned the up-to-date remedy in her first aid course, ran to the kitchen for baking soda. With tears of frustration streaming down their faces, they basted Peter until he looked as if he were ready for the oven, stopping only when he joined in my laughter.

We put up uncomplainingly with the small inconveniences of the home front. In a burst of patriotism we sold our car when gas rationing began, and managed well with our coupons for meat, coffee, and shoes, scorning the black market. Our only sacrifice was butter. With U.S. supplies going to the armed forces, civilians had to content themselves with margarine. Fearful that the public might become accustomed to the cheaper spread, the powerful dairy lobby had regulations passed that forbade margarine manufacturers from coloring their product. The margarine we bought was an unappetizing dead white, which was colored at home with red crystals that came in the package. Only after concerns about cholesterol surfaced decades later were the regulations against margarine rescinded.

Eating streaked margarine mattered little as we followed the progress of the war. The mighty German Army, which had overrun Europe, was bogged down on the eastern front. In Stalingrad, the Russians fought street by street, house by house, until in January 1943, the Germans were forced to surrender. With this first German defeat in four years of fighting, Russian popularity in the United States soared. Thousands contributed to Russian War Relief, joined the Council of American-Soviet Friendship, and flocked to see the films that Phil was publicizing. *Life* published a special issue devoted to the Soviet Union. The cover photograph by Margaret Bourke White showed Stalin, benevolent and smiling, looking like everyone's favorite grandfather. Inside were reports on the people of the USSR, a biography of Lenin, and sketches of current Soviet leaders. The Russians, said *Life*, were "one hell of a people" who "look like Americans, dress like Americans and think like Americans."

While Party members basked in the unaccustomed praise for things Russian, we continued to urge an Allied invasion of Europe that would decrease pressure on the Red Army. In Sunnyside, housewives set up tables on Queens Boulevard to collect signatures on petitions urging a Second Front. There were no comparable petitions asking the president to rescue Europe's six million Jews. Reports of Hitler's Final Solution for the Jews reached President Roosevelt and the State Department as early as 1942. The *New York Times* published an occasional article about death camps on page 11 or page 18, never on page 1. With official Washington soft-pedaling the story, the communist press, intent on winning support for the Soviet Union, paid scant attention to the plight of the Jews.

As a careful reader, I could have known—should have known—what was happening, but the Russians were first on my agenda. Not until the summer of 1944 did I really become aware of the Nazis' extermination program. I was at home on maternity leave when I read Time-Life correspondent Richard Lauterbach's report on the concentration camp at Maidenek, which the Red Army had just freed. Dick Lauterbach was a friend who had gone to P.S. 165 and who often stopped by my desk when he was in New York. His story in *Time* described Maidenek's gas chambers and crematoria, the mountain of bone and ashes, the warehouse full of shoes. Suddenly the unbelievable story became believable. Eight months later, when the Allied armies entered Auschwitz, Dachau, Buchenwald, and the other camps, we shivered at *Life's* photographs of the living skeletons in tattered clothing who emerged to greet the soldiers. Still, it was not until after the Nuremberg and Eichmann trials that I grasped the enormity of the Holocaust and felt my own ties to the Jewish people. Ashamed of the anti-Semitism I had grown up with, I began to root for the new state of Israel—even when the Party line decreed otherwise.

The future looked rosy for the world when Roosevelt, Churchill, and Stalin met in Teheran and agreed to "work together in the war and the peace that will follow." Their smiling faces, recorded by newsreel cameramen, promised a postwar world where capitalism and socialism would coexist. For the first time since the Nazi-Soviet pact, thousands of Americans joined the Party. Communist influence in the trade unions grew, and two communists were even elected to New York's City Council. Communist General Secretary Earl Browder was one of the many who believed that the Teheran agreement was a turning point in history. To sustain the wartime unity, he proposed converting the Communist Party into a Communist Political Association, which would function as an educational organization while supporting Roosevelt and the new American Labor Party. Although there was disagreement among the top leadership about this change, these debates scarcely reached ordinary members—and I was too preoccupied with my second pregnancy to pay much attention. However, I do recall the meeting of our shop unit when the Communist Political Association was presented as an accomplished fact. None of us questioned the functionary who brought us the news until he handed out individual membership cards, which we were to carry in our wallets at all times. Party membership had always been kept more or less secret. You might tell your best friends, but you certainly did not tell your boss or the members of a rival faction in the union. An employer who tolerated a suspected communist would feel obliged to fire him if he publicly admitted membership in the Party. Similarly, a trade union coalition could be left of center, but if its leader declared that he was a Party member—and therefore under the direction of 13th Street or Moscow—liberal supporters would drift away. In the wake of Teheran, perhaps Browder was right and it was time to end this secrecy and publicly proclaim, "I am a communist." But none of us, well-paid employees of Time Inc., activists in the ongoing struggle for control of the New York Newspaper Guild, were prepared to make the disclosure. To demonstrate our opposition to Browder's new line, we crowded into the bathroom, tore up the new membership cards, and solemnly flushed them down the toilet. That was the closest I ever came to carrying a Party card.

Within weeks of the formation of the Communist Political Association, the Allies landed in Normandy and the defeat of Hitler seemed inevitable. We cheered each advance, mourned each setback, and supported the Democrats in the fall election. On a rainy day in late October, when the president rode through New York in an open touring car, I took Peter to Queens Boulevard, lifting him to my shoulders so that he could see the great man. Two weeks later I cast my first vote for Franklin D. Roosevelt.

Nothing had shaken my belief that socialism was the best hope for mankind and that the survival of the world's first socialist state was of paramount importance. I still hoped to see a Soviet America some day. But the most absorbing event of my life that year was the birth of our daughter, Anne, on July 30, 1944. My obstetrician was a Park Avenue doctor who was also *Life's* medical advisor and a leader of the physicians' division of Russian War Relief. Because he knew me from the office, he treated me without the "There, there, little girl" condescension most obstetricians maintained toward their patients. But when he learned of my previous attempt at breastfeeding, he immediately vetoed the idea and after Anne's birth gave me a pill to dry up my milk supply. Feeling myself an old hand at mothering, I had no need for a baby nurse. With Annette's help and an occasional assist from Phil,

Anne and I quickly settled into a routine. She was as enchanting as Peter had been, and an easier baby to take care of, but I was ready to return to work when my maternity leave ended.

CHAPTER

8

So many men were in the armed forces that women at
Time-Life were given minor executive jobs. ("We let
down the bars," said a writer.) When I returned to
work I was appointed assistant chief in *Life*'s News
Bureau. An Associated Press teletype chattered in the
corridor, but the magazine's main news sources were
the bureau offices in major cities and a network of free-
lance journalists who covered stories in their areas.
Life's Bureau Chief was Helen Robinson, one of the
few other women on the magazine with a husband and
a child. With a staff of typists, we sat in a large bull pen
at the south end of the 31st floor, a favorite stopping-
off place for correspondents visiting the home office.

The atmosphere was informal, although the pace
was often hectic. All domestic stories outside of New
York funneled through the News Bureau. We parceled
out story suggestions from out-of-town offices and distributed the Washington newsletter, prized not only
for its gossipy anecdotes but for the reports labeled
"Confidential—Not for Attribution." Helen and I
attended the Newsfront conference, presided over by

the managing editor, where the stories to appear in the magazine that week were decided on.

We were also responsible for seeing that a censor's stamp was affixed to every photograph from the war front. Usually Helen, who worked the Tuesday–Saturday week, took care of this, but once on a Monday when I was in charge I found that a full-page picture of a Japanese officer, samurai sword raised to behead a kneeling Allied flier, lacked a censor's stamp. When I informed the managing editor of the problem it was almost a case of kill-the-messenger. Not only was this a unique illustration of a Japanese war crime, but the picture had come from Clare Booth Luce, who had just returned from a tour of the Pacific theater. Undoubtedly she had signed a statement promising to submit all photographs to censorship but had failed to honor her agreement. I was afraid that I would be ordered to the Waldorf Towers to confront the boss's wife, but we settled instead for a courier to Washington. The photograph came back the next day with the proper authorization.

The advantage of working in an all-female department became apparent in the last months of the war when Peter, ill with a kidney infection, was hospitalized so that he could be treated with the new wonder drug, penicillin. Family leave was unheard of, but I was able to go to the office in the morning and parcel out the assignments on my desk to sympathetic News

Bureau staffers before taking the bus to the hospital. In the late afternoon I returned to work to clear up the loose ends, then rushed home to nine-month-old Anne.

I can date Peter's illness with precision because one afternoon an older boy, radio in hand, shouted across the ward, "The president is dead!" On the bus going back to the office, driver and passengers alike had tears streaming down their faces. Even though I had perceived Roosevelt as too slow, too middle-of-the-road, too ready to compromise, the reforms brought about during his twelve years in office—social security, unemployment insurance, collective bargaining, farm supports—had altered the character of the nation. And I would always remember his handsome face, head thrown back in laughter, and his mellifluous voice as he opened fireside chats with "My friends."

I didn't feel that way about Earl Browder, the United States Communist leader, a mousy sort of man with a forgettable face and manner. Perhaps that is why I experienced little emotion when he was jobbed soon after FDR's death. I say "jobbed" because I now realize that he was ousted from his post on orders from Moscow, with the support of European communist leaders and his opponents in the United States. The people who had the least to say were the rank-and-file Party members. Once again we went through the motions, spending a Tuesday evening or two listening to the reports from Party headquarters. Had the

Communist Political Association been a "notorious revision of Marxism"? The answer was clearly "yes." In July 1945, a scant two months after the first public attack on Browder, the American Communist Party was reestablished with aging William Z. Foster as its chairman. Browder was expelled from the Party seven months later.

One or two friends were disturbed by this abrupt shift in line, but for most of us the world was moving at such breathtaking speed that we had little time for sectarian concerns. In April, representatives of fifty nations met in San Francisco to draw up a charter listing their common aims. "We, the Peoples of the United Nations" agreed on the need for peace, human rights, and social and economic progress. The ink was scarcely dry on the U.N. charter when American and Russian soldiers embraced at the Elbe River, seventy-five miles from Berlin. Mussolini was assassinated, Hitler a suicide, and, on May 7, the German Army formally surrendered.

For the first time in several years, Phil felt able to take a vacation. We rented a cottage on a sand dune overlooking Wellfleet Bay. Phil taught himself to sail a boat, using a Boy Scout manual borrowed from the library, and took movies of Anne as she staggered across the beach for her first encounter with salt water. Peter, who managed to keep afloat with a maximum of splashing, spent low-tide hours on the flats with me, sharing my fascination with hermit crabs, whelks, and Wellfleet oysters. We were eating supper in our tiny kitchen when the radio brought news that an atom bomb had been exploded over the Japanese city of Hiroshima. Atom bomb? No one knew the phrase. We eagerly combed the issues of the *New York Times* that managed to make it to the Lower Cape, learning that the bomb was the most fearsome weapon of destruction ever developed. After a second bomb was dropped on Nagasaki, then came word of the Japanese surrender. The terrible war was over at last.

Back home, people discarded blackout curtains and ration books and welcomed the returning soldiers. With my usual optimism I believed that when the great American war machine was converted to peacetime production, there would be goods enough for all. Hadn't Commerce Secretary Henry Wallace promised "a quart of milk for every person in the world"? Americans with milk aplenty would soon have washing machines, cars, new housing, and schools. My mood was enhanced when, after Phil's Artkino job ended, he found work in the publicity department of the Columbia Broadcasting System, his first good job in private industry since the early days of the Depression.

There were glimpses of trouble ahead. Slowly we realized that the atom bomb was not simply a bigger bomb but a scarcely conceivable weapon whose radiation could contaminate and kill for an incalculable period. And while the United States was the only country to possess the bomb in 1945, our monopoly would not last forever. It was only a matter of time before other countries developed the technology that would permit them to unlock the energy of the atom. That fall, Secretary of War Henry Stimson proposed that atomic energy be developed under U.N. auspices, but Soviet suspicions and U.S. intransigence killed the chance for peaceful development and the world was committed to a half-century of nuclear proliferation from which it has not yet recovered.

No one could foretell the future, although many tried. After a Soviet economist predicted another worldwide depression, we received a visit from a neighbor offering financial advice. A Marxist stock-broker—there were several on Wall Street in 1945—he not only accepted the Russians' pessimistic prognostication but saw a way to make money out of it—by selling short. I knew just enough about the workings of the stock market to grasp what he meant. Short-selling appealed as a way of taking advantage of "the contradictions of capitalism," a popular phrase in Party circles. If we agreed with the Soviet analysis of the future of the economy, we couldn't lose. Or could we? We withdrew our small savings from the bank, sold shares of stock recommended by our comrade broker, then bought them back again, making a few hundred dollars' profit. But we lacked the nerves of steel required for this way of making money and deep down we did not believe in the Soviet prophecy of doom. During our adult lives we had known only depression and war. Now we shared the postwar dream of peace and plenty and, with our friends, the Ehrenbergs and Wrights, made plans to move to the suburbs.

Ann Ehrenberg and her husband, Mike, a photographer, lived a few doors down the street. She and I had met through our obstetrician when I was pregnant with Peter and she with her daughter, Devera. Henry Wright, now managing editor of the *Architectural Forum*, and his wife, Dorothy, had moved to Sunnyside after the birth of their second child. Not only had we all outgrown our Sunnyside houses, but we were concerned about the inadequate schools that our children would soon attend. Although suburban homes were available at depression prices, we never considered buying a ready-made house. We looked forward to modern homes with picture windows and shed roofs, like those pictured in *The Forum*. Besides, Westchester had a reputation of being rock-ribbed Republican. Mindful of our Pelham experience, we wanted to live near each other, creating our own congenial neighborhood.

We looked at land in several towns before an ad in the Sunday *Times* offered nineteen wooded acres in Rye for $1,000 an acre. The land was breathtaking —

hilly, rocky, with hundred-year-old trees. Adjacent to Grace Church Street, a neighborhood of pillared Colonial mansions and manicured lawns, the property even included rights to a small beach on Long Island Sound, ten minutes away. Everything checked out. Rye, a city of 15,000, was an express stop on the New Haven Railroad, only thirty-eight minutes from Grand Central Station. Its Main Street included two book-stores and one of the new A&P supermarkets; its schools were reputed to be excellent.

Of course we couldn't manage nineteen acres, but it proved easy to find other couples to go along with us. In late December 1945 we purchased the property, planning to develop eight acres, then sell off the remainder. Allan Woodle, a former *Forum* writer, became our contractor, while Henry and an engineer member of the group laid out a dead-end road and sub-divided the land. Because no one wanted houses in neat rows, they drew boundaries conforming to the features of the property so that the lots varied in size, some level, some hilly. How were we to decide who got which lot? To be fair, I suggested that we put the lot numbers in a hat and pick blindly. I admit to a slight twinge of regret when the lot we picked was the hilliest and thus the most difficult to build on.

Our idealism was tested again early in 1946 when Henry called an emergency meeting. He had just returned from Washington, where he had learned that the Federal Housing Administration was about to declare a moratorium on home building. So great was the pent-up demand for new homes, and so severe the shortage of materials, that after April 1 only war veterans would be allowed to build. Anyone who had so much as a shovel in the ground before then could continue; otherwise they must wait an indefinite period until the ban was lifted. Should we take advantage of Henry's insider knowledge and begin to excavate? Unanimously we decided that the veterans came first. We would wait. It was a decision that cost us a lot in dollars and in comfort.

Meanwhile we went ahead with the road, named Kirby Lane North, and had our first intimation of why no developer had tackled this parcel before. Underneath its green cover was solid mica schist, requiring the road contractor to blast every foot of the way. Then a well-digger had to drill up to a thousand feet below the surface to find water. Adding the expense of the road and the wells, each $1,000 lot now cost between $6,000 and $8,000. We borrowed money from Dad's bank at a low interest rate and kept on smiling.

Henry used the hiatus to design our houses. Because Phil and I wanted ours to be at ground level despite the hilly site, he patiently fitted in rooms, ramps, and steps until we had a house of seven levels. It was ingenious—and expensive. At the time the FHA moratorium had gone into effect, building costs had been $8 to $10 a square foot. When wartime price controls were lifted, the cost of building materials doubled and tripled; double-glazing specified for our floor-to-ceiling windows quintupled. Happily ignorant of the meaning of heat loss, we canceled the double-glazing and settled for single panes of glass. For the next twenty years, guests visiting in winter kept their coats on.

Nor was this our only poor decision. Of course we wanted radiant heating, a new concept touted by *The Forum* that warmed the objects in a room directly rather than heating the air as convection heating did. Henry's design, one of the first in the country, called for heating pipes in the ceiling covered by metal panels. As water of varying temperature flowed through the pipes, they expanded and contracted, gurgling, burbling, and beating a rat-tat-tat. The banging was a conversation-stopper in the living room and awakened even the heaviest sleeper immediately.

In 1946, Eric Hodgins, a *Fortune* editor, wrote *Mr. Blandings Builds His Dream House*, a best-seller that chronicled the adventures of a New York couple who built a house in the country. Taken by a wily real estate man, swindled by a local law firm, and bilked by a slick contractor, their $20,000 house cost them $56,263. Yet when they saw it on a spring day, "floating on a sea of mud," "a cry of joy" escaped them. "The house was lovelier than the fairest drawings" their architect had made.

We laughed at the misadventures of the Blandings, but they were too close for comfort. When we moved to Rye on April 1, 1948 (April Fool's Day!), we were seriously in debt. We too plodded through a sea of mud demarking our not-yet paved driveway and balanced precariously on living room floor joists as we waited for the flooring contractor. We looked out at a hill of rubble that would be a terrace someday.

But we had no wily villains to blame. Dad had done our legal work without charge. Henry and Allan Woodle worked hard with little profit to themselves. Postwar inflation and our mutual inexperience were responsible for our plight. More than half a century later, I asked Ann Ehrenberg why none of us had criticized Henry for the problems, financial and other, that our houses had brought us. "Because we all thought he was a genius," she said. And I agreed.

Our house was beautiful. It really looked like the houses in the *Architectural Forum,* which published pictures of it the following year. Exterior walls were of fieldstone; inside, every window looked out on trees, wildflowers, and rocky knolls. A slatted overhang permitted the sun to flood the rooms in winter but kept them cool and shaded on summer days. No matter that we owed Dad's bank more than twice as much as anticipated and could barely keep up with the payments. There were bluejays nesting in a tree bordering the driveway, and pheasants marched majestically up the hill to eat the cracked corn I put outside.

During the years of planning and building I was so absorbed in questions of design that I almost reverted to my college art-for-art's-sake days. Lunch hours were spent selecting paint colors, hunting for drapery materials and furniture. When Artek, the store that imported Alvar Aalto's designs, had a sale, I bought one hundred bentwood legs in assorted sizes, sharing them with the neighbors. We still have tables and chairs like those in the Museum of Modern Art's 1998 retrospective of Aalto's work.

However, I could never fully lose myself in aesthetics. My job was demanding and so were the children. Anne had become a beguiling person of her own, joining Peter and me on our Saturday excursions. We ate our first-ever pizzas in the neighboring town of Port Chester, which had a large Italian population, and picked violets and crabapple blossoms on our road.

Along with these pleasant preoccupations, politics remained in the foreground. The dream of a peaceful postwar world that had sent us hunting for land in the suburbs had faded rapidly. The unity proclaimed by the Big Three at Teheran gave way to an Iron Curtain that divided Europe. The Cold War was under way. Before work had begun on our house, Truman had established a Loyalty Review Board requiring every government employee to declare that he was not and had never been a member of the communist party. Those of us who had grown up during the Left–New Deal coalition could not believe that an anti-Communist hysteria could develop or that it would transform American institutions. When Henry Wallace, vice-president during Roosevelt's third term, challenged Truman's "get tough" policy and called for "friendly peaceful competition" between nations, we gratefully supported him as candidate of the Progressive Party in the 1948 election. None of Wallace's followers expected him to win, but the hope was that he would poll enough votes to demonstrate the strength of a pro-peace movement. On Election Day he ran a poor third.

Although I still failed to grasp the strength of the anti-communist forces, I could see them at work at union meetings, where conservatives, Trotskyists, and members of the Association of Catholic Trade Unions banded together to oust the left-wingers. The struggle in the Newspaper Guild mirrored similar battles in other unions. After Congress passed the Taft-Hartley Act, which required union officials to sign affidavits stating that they were not members of the communist party, the CIO pledged that its leaders would not sign. But as fear of Soviet expansion grew, the CIO capitulated, purging the left unions, which had been the main strength of progressive forces in the United States.

Time and *Life* had never had a liberal editorial policy, but now *Time*'s foreign news stories reflected an evangelical anti-Communism that was noticeably different from the reporting in the *New York Times* and other papers. As correspondents returned from their posts abroad, they stopped in the News Bureau to tell us what was happening. No matter what stories John Hersey sent from Moscow, Charles Wertenbaker from Paris, or Theodore White from China, *Time* Foreign News editor Whittaker Chambers rewrote their accounts. I only knew Chambers as a pudgy, disheveled man who occasionally attended Guild meetings, but the correspondents and researchers who worked with him filled me in on his background. A contributor to the *Daily Worker* and *New Masses* and a Communist courier in the 1930s, he had broken with the Party and had come to work for *Time*, evolving into the company's leading anti-communist. Week after week, he tossed aside the cables from correspondents overseas and rewrote their reports. When a researcher refused to check his version of the news he shrugged his shoulders and said, "Truth doesn't matter." His mission was to convince *Time*'s readers that the Soviet Union's goal was "the conquest of the free world."

Complaints about Chambers's distortions of the news became so numerous that editorial director John Shaw Billings instituted a formal inquiry. Time correspondents around the world were queried, and the chief Foreign News researcher checked a year's cables against published articles. Although her report proved the truth of the correspondents' charges, Henry Luce declared that Chambers had been doing "a fine job" and left him in charge of Foreign News.

In addition to its support of Chambers, Time management reflected the nation's preoccupation with the Red hunt in other ways. A *Time* researcher, Blanche Finn, formerly a communist but now strongly anti, was assigned to attend the Jefferson School and other left-wing study groups. She collected letterheads of left-of-center organizations and clipped the *Daily Worker* to set up a card file of people who could be called communists or party liners without fear that the magazines would be sued. Herbert Solow, a *Fortune* editor who had moved from Zionism to Communism to Trotskyism in the 30s, became the company's expert on internal Communism. In a 1948 memo he proposed ways to ferret out staff radicals. "Assign work without respect to personal (political) tastes," he advised. "There is no reason why, under proper supervision, a known C.P. member should not research, write or edit a piece about Trotsky, Stalin's dealings with Ribbentrop, Browder's current status. When handling a suspect's copy the editors must confront him with his questionable statements, thereby eliciting illuminating psychological factors (sincerity, surprise, defiance, confusion, deviousness, functional stomachache or whatever). A few lessons of that kind and an active Stalinist would wonder whether it wouldn't be better to quit."

Herbert Solow's proposal, which was duly filed in the morgue, was never put into practice. At that time few *Time* or *Life* writers belonged to the communist shop unit. However, foreign correspondents' views continued to differ from Henry Luce's. In the past there had never been a penalty for expressing differences, but in the overheated atmosphere of the late 40s, staff writers were required to submit their outside writing for approval. If they persisted in publishing views that differed from *Time*'s, they could be fired.

When Richard Lauterbach refused to make changes in his manuscript of *Danger from the East*, based on a tour of the USSR, Japan, and China, he came to my desk to say goodbye. I also had visits from Theodore White, *Time-Life* correspondent in China and a favorite of Luce's until he became too critical of Chiang Kai-Shek. Teddy was in New York working with his assistant, Annalee Jacoby, on *Thunder over China*, a book made up in large part from their unpublished *Time* dispatches. Shortly before the book's publication, Luce informed him that he was "too objective" and that "the time for objectivity is past." When Teddy refused to take any job Luce assigned to him, he too was fired. He stopped to see me later that day, his round face wreathed in smiles. He had just learned that *Thunder* was a Book-of-the-Month Club selection. Although the book was banned in China, it became a best-seller in the United States, the first of many that Teddy was to write.

I was too low on the Time Inc. totem pole to feel threatened by the company's new hard line. However, I had begun to think seriously about leaving *Life*. Commuting from Rye was more of a strain than I had anticipated. The express train was often late, lengthening the hours I was away from Peter and Anne. Moreover, my work had become routine, and as men returned from the army our little fiefdom in the News Bureau was threatened. When Helen Robinson was fired, I felt sure that the man replacing her would treat me as a glorified clerk. However, leaving Time Inc, after twelve years was not a step to be taken lightly. Much as I deplored the company's editorial policy, I was earning $116 a week, a salary that would be hard to match elsewhere.

After tentative discussions with my new boss and with the personnel department, I discovered that the company would be as glad to replace me with a man as I would be to leave. To sweeten my departure, they offered me a year's pay, four months more than the severance pay required under the Guild contract. Although I was terrified at the thought of job hunting again, it was mutually agreed that I would leave on April 30, 1949.

Before departing, I had work to do. Whenever correspondents and photographers stopped at my desk to swap tales of the sometimes funny, sometimes outrageous things that happened, someone would inevitably say, "That's one for the book." What book? Why, the book about Time Inc, that one of us was going to write some day. I had not thought of doing it myself—I was a researcher, not a writer—but I had a bulging file of company memos and reports from the Washington Bureau, and I spent lunch hours transcribing the cables correspondents had sent from abroad to compare with Whittaker Chambers's rewrites. Chambers was front-page news in 1948–49 after he testified before the House Un-American Activities Committee that Alger Hiss, a former State Department official, who played a prominent role at the founding meeting of the United Nations, had been a communist spy. I did not know Hiss, but when a friend of his asked me to talk with his lawyers I shared with them the information on Chambers that I had collected. My report added to their psychological profile of Chambers, but it did not save Hiss from a perjury conviction and jail sentence.

Happy to be at home with the children, I slowly began to assemble the Time Inc. material I had gathered. A Rye acquaintance arranged a meeting with Cedric Belfrage, a talented British journalist now living in the United States, who might be available to collaborate with me. Belfrage was interested, but as a co-founder of the *National Guardian*, a new progressive weekly, he had little free time. If I would complete and organize the research, he agreed to do a rewrite job. That summer I drove to Connecticut to talk to John Hersey, and to Long Island to see Charles Wertenbaker, former *Time-Life* chief of foreign correspondents. I made trips to New York to lunch with *Time* writers and researchers who contributed to accounts of Chambers's devious personality, and talked with Corinne Thrasher, Luce's secretary, to learn details of her boss's 12 to 16-hour work day. I even drove through the grounds of the Luces' estate in Greenwich, but lacked the courage to knock on their front door.

In the fall of 1949, when Anne entered kindergarten and Peter fourth grade, I went to work in earnest, going through every issue of *Time*, *Life*, and *Fortune* from their beginnings as well as reading Time's annual reports to learn the company's financial underpinnings. The more attentively I read, the more I became convinced that the leading stories in the magazines were tailored to support Henry Luce's friends, confound his enemies, and forward his vision of the 20th century as the American Century, when the United States would wrest control of world markets from Great Britain and other competitors. To illustrate the way that *Time*'s style was used to bolster its editors' biases, I found a 1948 *Time* article on Henry Wallace that employed almost a dozen pejoratives—awkward, disheveled, shambling, brooding, erratic, sour, weak, embittered, helpless—to convince readers that Wallace could not be trusted.

In addition to chapters on Chambers, Luce, the Republican Party, and the China lobby, I included many of the entertaining anecdotes that my friends and I had been relishing for a decade. Because I was assembling research for Cedric Belfrage and not for publication, the writing went quickly. In the spring of 1950, I gave Belfrage more than three hundred manuscript pages, which I had titled *It's About Time*. To my surprise, he returned them to me a few days later with a smile. "You've written your book," he said.

Although I could scarcely believe him, I packed up the manuscript and mailed it to Simon and Schuster. The editors rejected it, but a day or two later I received a telephone call from Mavis McIntosh, one of New York's leading literary agents. Someone at Simon and Schuster had told her about the manuscript. After reading it, she took me on as a client. As *It's About Time* made the rounds of publishers, a strange interlude began for Mavis and me.

An editor at Little Brown told her that the firm wanted the book, but then abruptly returned it. Doubleday agreed to publish it, but rejected it two days later. A Viking editor asked me to come to New

York so that she could suggest revisions. I made the changes she asked for, but she turned the book down. For months I continued to meet with editors at Harcourt Brace, Athenaeum, and other publishers whose names I no longer remember. Always there was initial interest and then a rejection. Speculating that the publishers were afraid of retaliation from *Time* and *Life*, Mavis regretfully returned the manuscript. Even after she relinquished it, an editor at Julian Messner tried to work out a collaboration with A. J. Liebling, author of the *New Yorker*'s prestigious "Wayward Press" column. If he would co-author the book, his name would give it the authority that mine lacked. When this too fell through, I put the manuscript in a file drawer and went on with my life.

Three decades later, when I obtained my FBI file under the provisions of the Freedom of Information Act, I finally discovered what had hit me. Most of the forty-odd pages from the Bureau were blacked out, presumably to protect the identity of informers, but one page was largely intact. Dated December 28, 1950, it was a memo from L. B. Nichols, the Bureau's assistant director, to Clyde Tolson, J. Edgar Hoover's closest friend. "BLANK called and wondered if we could be of some assistance. He states that BLANK BLANK BLANK has an excellent manuscript written by Dorothy Sterling for *Time* magazine which does a good job. It is a very fascinating and readable document. BLANK is concerned about Dorothy Sterling's background. I told BLANK after I checked that of course we could not divulge anything from the files but that BLANK BLANK BLANK should be very careful what they did about Dorothy Sterling. She was enrolled in the Communist Party on the election registration of 1936. She married Philip Sterling who was employed in 1942 and 1943 by Artkino Pictures."

Still another decade passed before I learned that Time Inc. had also been involved in suppressing the manuscript. When Robert Herzstein was writing his definitive biography *Henry R. Luce*, he found an entry in John Shaw Billings's diary, by then on file in the University of South Carolina library. Managing editor of *Life* during most of my years on the magazine and later Time Inc. editorial director, Billings had written on January 10, 1951, "Jim Shepley [Time's Washington Bureau chief] called up to tell me that J. Edgar Hoover revealed that Dorothy Sterling, ex *Life* researcher was a Communist—a fact which so far has killed a scurrilous book by her on Time Inc. and Luce."

I was not surprised to learn that *Time* executives had worked with the FBI to kill my book. One of my points in writing *It's About Time* had been to describe the management's reactionary policies. But I was profoundly shocked to discover that major book publishers had turned to J. Edgar Hoover for a report on me.

This kind of hand holding with the FBI was new to the publishing world in 1950.

It's About Time is hopelessly dated today. But as the first full-length study of the Luce empire, it contained a considerable amount of fresh information. Since no less a critic than the FBI's L. B. Nichols described it as "excellent, fascinating and readable," it had the potential of becoming a best-seller. And then what direction would my life have taken?

CHAPTER

9

When Mavis McIntosh returned the manuscript of *It's About Time,* she confirmed my belief that I was not a writer. For a few heady months I had dared to dream that I could become an investigative reporter and comment on the national scene. But with the string of rejections, the self-doubts stemming from the Time experience of writer-male, researcher-female took over again. I had no question about continuing to work. Not only was my income needed, but I had little interest in such pursuits as home decorating and cake baking, which were beginning to absorb my neighbors. But what could I work at without commuting to New York?

The answer came soon after I formulated the question. Surely every mother has said to herself when reading to her children, "I can write as well as *that* author." Before I had a chance to investigate writing children's books, our dachshund, Sophie, had a litter of puppies on Anne's bed. The puppies were so beguiling, the children who came to play with them so attractive, that photographer Mike Ehrenberg went to work to record the story. As I devised a simple narrative, he photographed the dogs' development until we had a book. Because the collaboration went smoothly, we then took young Billy Wright for a spring walk through fields and woods and brought *Sophie and Her Puppies* and *Billy Takes a Walk* to a children's book editor in New York.

Unlike Time's male-dominated world, the editors of children's books—"baby books," they were called in the trade—were women. Margaret Lesser, who presided over Doubleday's Books for Young Readers, was a former journalist and working mother who accepted both books and encouraged Mike and me to go ahead with *Trees and Their Story*, a straightforward nature book that grew out of an article I had worked on for *Life*. All three were selections of the Junior Literary Guild, a Doubleday subsidiary.

Photographic books for children were a novelty in the early 1950s. After we had finished *Trees*, Peggy Lesser asked us for a book on the shiny new United Nations buildings along the East River. We spent weeks wandering through the Secretariat building, discovering a fully equipped fire department and post office, print shop and medical clinic, and photographing a meeting of the Security Council. In the text I emphasized the diversity of the representatives of the ninety-nine nations and their devotion to world peace.

Close to My Heart

While working on *United Nations, N.Y.*, I also struck out in a new direction, trying my hand at mystery stories. *The Cub Scout Mystery*, written while Peter was a Cub Scout, and *The Brownie Scout Mystery*, after Anne became a Brownie, were followed by *The Silver Spoon Mystery* and *The Secret of the Old Post Box*. The books were set in suburban communities resembling Rye, the characters based on my children and their friends. The unstated moral was that if the youngsters worked together, using their wits, they could solve mysteries that baffled the grownups around them. From a literary point of view I thought them better than the Nancy Drew series, although they never matched her popularity.

Before long I had five books in print, but I still did not think of myself as a writer. Each morning as I sat down at the typewriter I told myself, "You're writing research for Joe Kastner." Only after I addressed a few sentences to him could I get going. I enjoyed the work but wanted to tackle something more challenging. My mind went back to Spec Op, to Dr. Hollingworth's biography class. Anne was reading widely now, working her way through the Rye Library's shelf of juvenile biographies, but scarcely any were about women. I decided to write a biography of a woman, a heroic figure who would say to girls, "You are as strong and capable as boys."

In the *Daily Worker* and *National Guardian* I had read about such people as Frederick Douglass, Sojourner Truth, and Harriet Tubman. I chose Harriet Tubman, leader of the Underground Railroad. From Earl Conrad's biography of her, written in 1943, I learned of the courage and ingenuity that had enabled her to bring more than three hundred slaves to freedom, her leadership of guerrilla forces in South Carolina during the Civil War, and her long career afterward as a champion of her people and advocate of women's rights. Tubman lived until 1913, the year that I was born. Why had I never heard of her in school or college? Why was her name unfamiliar to everyone I knew?

My search for Harriet Tubman led me to the Schomburg Collection (now the Schomburg Center for Research in Black Culture), in a dingy building on 135th Street in Harlem. Schomburg's books, newspapers, and manuscripts were a revelation. Here was the whole hidden history of black people: newspapers dating back to 1827, letters from blacks during the colonial period and later, accounts of slave escapes and rebellions, paintings, sculpture and an extensive collection of Negro spirituals and work songs. I also found books and newspapers by abolitionists who sympathized with their black sisters and brothers.

Walking through Harlem from the railroad station at 125th Street was also an education. I had learned a little about New York's black city within a city from Annette, our former housekeeper who had told us how, as a parochial school pupil, she had been forbidden to march in the St. Patrick's Day parade with her white classmates. She was living with us when she tried unsuccessfully to obtain a bank loan to buy a car. I interceded for her at my bank, but the loan officer bluntly told me, "We don't loan money to colored people." After I took out a loan in my own name, she bought the car but could not obtain insurance for it. Only when she registered the car from our address was she able to buy a policy.

I tried different routes from the station, passing "the lung block," where the tuberculosis rate was twice as high as in the rest of the city, then walking along Strivers Row, a tree-lined street whose well-kept houses had been designed by architect Stanford White in the 1890s. I stopped to look at the impressive Abyssinian Baptist Church, whose pastor, Adam Clayton Powell, Jr., was a U.S. congressman, bought copies of the *Amsterdam News* and the *New York Age*, black newspapers, at newsstands along Eighth Avenue, and books at the National Memorial Book Store at the corner of 125th Street. It was there that I found *Scenes in the Life of Harriet Tubman*, an as-told-to biography taken down by a white woman in 1869, and William Still's *The Underground Railroad*, a first-hand report of the travelers on the road, published in 1871.

These books were the beginning of our extensive collection on black history and life.

The staff at Schomburg were friendly. Curator Jean Blackwell Hutson, who had attended Barnard when I did but had not been permitted to live in a dormitory, gave me space to set up my typewriter in an upstairs room close to the stacks. Over lunch she told me stories about W. E. B Du Bois, who had recently married her childhood friend, Shirley Graham. They were the kind of stories that women exchange about men whom they admire but find exasperating. Du Bois was something of a dandy who felt underdressed without gloves and walking stick. He also insisted on a ceremony for making the "perfect" cup of coffee: correct pot, exact measurements of water, and specially ground coffee—that Jean thought amusing. On other days, Ernest Kaiser, Schomburg's expert bibliographer, shared a cafeteria tray with me at the Harlem YMCA cafeteria down the street, where I was often the only white person.

My excitement about the black experience carried over when I sat down to write. For the first time I wrote with ease, not feeling the need to invoke a male mentor. I finished the book in about six months and then waited impatiently for Doubleday to bring it out. The photographic books and *Cub Scout Mystery* had been published within a year of completion. *Freedom Train: The Story of Harriet Tubman* languished at Books for Young Readers for more than two years, the delay doubtless caused by the fear, prevalent in publishing circles, that books about black people would not sell. When Peggy Lesser finally telephoned to say that they were going ahead with the book, I suggested that it be illustrated by a black artist. The art department turned up Ernest Crichlow, who had illustrated *Two Is a Team*, the first and for a long time the only "integrated" picture book. On the rare occasions when black people had been depicted in children's books they had been shown with light skins and Anglo-Saxon features or as Sambo-like caricatures. Crichlow's Harriet Tubman was a strong woman, unmistakably African-American. A pleasant by-product of our collaboration on *Freedom Train* was that Ernest and I became friends. With his wife and small son, he visited us in Rye, and Phil and I traveled to the Fort Greene neighborhood in Brooklyn where they lived in a remodeled brownstone.

Although *Freedom Train* was not a selection of the Junior Literary Guild, it was favorably reviewed, particularly in the black press. Evelyn Cunningham, an enterprising reporter for the *Pittsburgh Courier,* even located a grand-niece of Tubman's and brought us together for an interview and photographs. However, the book did not sell as well as my other books until the 1960s, when sales doubled and tripled. Today, more than forty years later, it is the only one of my early books still in print.

Writing at home was the ideal solution for a working mother. My study faced the road, so that in mid-afternoon when I heard Anne coming down the path, I stopped to give her milk and cookies, then went back to my typewriter until Peter arrived. I was available to drive them to school in bad weather—no school buses then—and to dentist and doctor appointments. If they were sick, I plumped up pillows and served chicken soup.

Working at home presented some problems, however. Advances for each book ranged from $375 to $500; it took more than a decade before my royalties equaled my *Life* salary. We quickly discovered that we could not afford to keep Annette. Although it was a wrench to have her leave, I managed well enough with a once-a-week cleaning woman—except for the cooking. There were no prepared foods, frozen vegetables, or takeout dishes available, and I had many disasters. Peter recalls Sunday mornings in Rye when "Mom burned the bacon and Dad yelled at her."

My family's sophisticated palates were not the only ones to consider. The 1950s, when "togetherness" was the watchword, were trying years for many women. With the leisure provided by such postwar marvels as washing machines and dryers they were expected to chauffeur their children to music lessons and little league games, to make their own draperies, knit sweaters, and serve gourmet meals. Dinners were no longer the meat 'n' potatoes of an earlier generation. When we dined with friends we were served elaborate casseroles, homemade bread, and multi-layered cakes. Even Alice, living in nearby Harrison with her husband and daughter and carving out a career as a writer for women's magazines, became a good cook. When we met for lunch, we exchanged recipes.

Another problem, which Alice shared, was that no one respected my working hours. Fuller Brush and Electrolux salesmen and earnest distributors of *The Watchword* beat a path to my door. The phone rang constantly with solicitations for the Lighthouse for the Blind or Our Lady of Sodality. When I asked a neighbor how she got rid of importunate salespeople, she was surprised at my lack of finesse. "I tell them that I have to ask my husband," she said. Somehow I had never thought of that.

Even more annoying than the salesmen were the calls from neighbors who phoned me at all hours to arrange a car pool, to ask for a cake for a PTA sale, or just to chat. The telephone traffic increased after I joined an informal group of second-grade mothers who were critical of the school principal, James Collins, a conservative who believed in corporal punishment, opposed hiring a school psychologist, and frightened the children with grisly reports on the Red Menace during weekly air raid drills. After he spanked one of Anne's classmates, the boy's mother asked me to accompany her to a school board meeting to protest. When the board voted to ban corporal punishment and later appointed a school psychologist, my phone rang even more often. Because I was just then discovering Harriet Tubman, I proposed a new way to improve the atmosphere of the school. Why not ask Mr. Collins to observe Negro History Week? In 1952 Negro History Week was ignored in Westchester schools, but the women acceded to my suggestion when the mother of the only black second grader joined our schoolyard discussions. Mrs. Brown, whose husband was president of the local NAACP, accompanied me to see Mr. Collins. He loftily informed us, "We do not teach Negro history or Chinese history. We teach American history." However, he agreed to a small exhibit in the library to mark Brotherhood Week. Developed by the National Council of Christians and Jews, Brotherhood Week seemed to me a watered-down version of Negro History Week, but we called on a Rye woman who worked for the Anti-Defamation League for help. She loaned us some books and pamphlets on interracial topics, which Mrs. Brown and I delivered to the school library. Several days later, I asked Peter, then a sixth grader, if his classmates had commented on the exhibit.

"What exhibit?" he replied. "There's nothing in the library." When I telephoned Mr. Collins, his voice was icy. "That wasn't Brotherhood Week material you brought in. That was communist propaganda," he said. Bewildered, I went to school to pick up the offending material. Mr. Collins was too busy to see me, but he placed an oversized paperback, *Peoples of the Earth*, by Edwin Embree, on top of the pile. *Peoples of the Earth* was an elaboration of *The Races of Mankind*, by anthropologists Ruth Benedict and Gene Weltfish, a pamphlet circulated during World War II by the Office of War Information. Embree, who had had a distinguished career as director of the Rockefeller Foundation and president of the Julius Rosenwald Fund, had traced the development of different races, concluding with a plea to end discrimination against Jews and Negroes in the United States. I had to read very carefully to find the passages that had upset Mr. Collins. On pages 48–49 Embree had written that white western civilization was losing its dominance because common people of the world were demanding equality. "This movement got a powerful lift from the Communist Revolution in Russia, where the people are building a great industrial power," he wrote. Never mind that his next sentence said, "Unhappily, the ruling oligarchy frankly declares itself a dictatorship and curbs liberties and ideas as sternly as an ancient despotism." Undoubtedly this was the communist propaganda that Collins had pounced on.

Immediately I phoned the half-dozen women who had been calling me every day, expecting amusement if

not indignation. Instead I was greeted with silence.
There were no phone calls from them the next morning. Or the day after, or the day after that. Except for
Mrs. Brown, they avoided me in the schoolyard. Only
once did a member of the group, the wife of an advertising executive, volunteer an explanation. When we
met on Main Street she said with some embarrassment, "My husband told me never to talk to you
again."

CHAPTER

10

On a Sunday afternoon in June 1950, more than a
year before l'Affaire Brotherhood, a friend and I
trudged along dimly lit corridors in an apartment
house in Port Chester. We were soliciting signatures
for the Stockholm Peace Appeal, which called for out-
lawing atomic weapons. The appeal was backed by
such international figures as Bertrand Russell, the
Joliot-Curies, Linus Pauling, and W. E. B. Du Bois,
but we felt diffident because radios were blaring from
every apartment and doors were slammed in our faces.
The atmosphere was so threatening that we cut short
our mission. From our car radio we learned that the
Korean War had begun.

My attempt to collect signatures for peace on the
day that President Truman initiated a "police action" in
Korea was yet another instance of my failure to grasp
the changing mood of the nation. In 1950, the Cold
War focused not only on the Soviet Union but on
American communists, not only on communists but on
fellow travelers, parlor pinks, socialists, and pacifists
as well. After the Russians exploded their first atom

bomb, J. Edgar Hoover declared that the secret of the bomb had been stolen, and directed the FBI to "find the thieves."

A year after we moved to Rye, anti-communist vigilantism came perilously close to home. Paul Robeson had scheduled a concert in Peekskill, a blue-collar city in western Westchester where New Yorkers, mostly Jewish, spent summer vacations. Robeson, a target of the Red hunters because he defended the Soviet Union and international peace, had sung in the Peekskill area for the past three years, but this time was different. Beforehand, members of the American Legion, Veterans of Foreign Wars, and the Chamber of Commerce called for "group action" to halt the concert. On the appointed day more than a thousand men and boys attacked concertgoers with clubs and rocks, smashed the stage, overturned cars. We listened anxiously to the radio as a newscaster described the twelve-foot cross that was set ablaze while rioters shouted "Kill the Commies" and "Dirty Kikes."

A hastily formed committee scheduled a second Robeson concert to be held three miles from Peekskill the following Sunday. While husky union men and a contingent of Spanish Civil War veterans came from New York to stand guard, virtually every man we knew in Westchester boarded a chartered bus headed for the concert grounds. Some armed themselves with baseball bats. When I kissed Phil goodbye I saw that he had buttoned a billet from our log pile inside his jacket.

I am amazed now that I was willing to stay home with the women and children while the men went off to do battle. At the concert, as Phil told me later, Paul Robeson sang "Ol' Man River" and "Let My People Go," while protesters on the perimeter of the crowd shouted "Go back to Russia, you niggers" and "Go home, you dirty Jews." Afterward, the police routed the departing cars down a steep winding road where gangs waited for them. The protesters hurled rocks at the passing vehicles, halting some to pull out passengers and beat them. Phil returned home at dusk, tired and disheveled. The windows of his bus had been smashed, but none of the passengers was hurt. Grimly he deposited his billet in the back of our coat closet, where it remained for years, a reminder of a violent day.

That week *Life* reported that the Communists had aimed for "the calculated, purposeful incitement of racial conflict" but failed to publish pictures taken by Cornell Capa, then a staff photographer, that showed Legionnaires and state troopers beating concert-goers. After a cursory investigation, Governor Thomas Dewey declared that the audience had been "followers of Red totalitarianism" and had "obviously provoked" the incident. New stickers appeared on Westchester cars: "COMMUNISM IS TREASON — BEHIND COMMUNISM STANDS THE JEWS."

Nine months after the Peekskill riot, government agents arrested Julius and Ethel Rosenberg, accusing them of giving the secret of the atom bomb to the Russians. Phil and I and most people we knew believed that they were the innocent victims of a frame-up, and I particularly sympathized with Ethel, only two years younger than I, and the mother of small children. Although recently released documents from the KGB files indicate that Julius did turn over military information—but not the secret of the atom bomb—to the Russians, I still believe that their trial was unfair, their lawyer inept, and the death sentence disproportionate to the crime they were accused of. Ethel Rosenberg was the first woman executed by the federal government since 1865 when Mary Surratt was hanged for complicity in the assassination of Abraham Lincoln.

For many months, the Rosenberg case dominated our lives. We read the pair's moving letters from the death house in Sing Sing, went to meetings called on their behalf in New York and drove to Washington to take part in a vigil in front of the White House. Despite pleas for clemency from Pope Pius XII and other notables, the date of their execution was set for June 19, 1953. After work that day, Phil went to Union Square where a crowd gathered, hoping for a last-minute reprieve. I was at home fixing supper when the telephone rang and a gloating voice said "The R-o-s-e-n-b-e-r-g-s a-r-e going to d-i-e!" The malice of the anonymous caller shook me. Telling Peter and Anne to take their supper, I fled from the house. Hardly knowing where I was going I drove to the beach, until I felt calmer. Returning home, I turned on the radio to hear the announcement: "Ethel and Julius Rosenberg are dead."

In the 1990s, when the KGB files were opened to western readers, we learned that the Rosenbergs had indeed been spies who gave secrets, though not the bomb, to the Russians. My first reaction was anger—all that wasted emotion—and those orphaned boys. But in retrospect, I see that Ethel—caring, idealistic Ethel—believed so strongly in the improbable, impossible dream of world socialism that she gave her life rather than risk tarnishing it. There is tragedy here that still needs pondering.

After the execution of the Rosenbergs, any prudent person would have recognized what was happening and would have left the Communist Party. But Phil and I were not prudent people. For all of our adult lives we had dreamed of ending poverty and racism. With atomic war too terrible to contemplate, peace had become the paramount issue. We knew from our own experience that there was no communist conspiracy to overthrow the government. On the contrary, we learned at Party meetings that our job was to win people over to our way of thinking in order to effect gradual change. In addition to these broader considerations, there was the code of honor that everyone learned in childhood: be loyal to your friends; don't squeal; don't desert in time of trouble.

The American Communist Party was clearly in trouble. From a war time high of 75,000, its membership had dwindled to 31,000, an infinitesimal number in a population of one hundred and fifty million. A few acquaintances had fallen by the wayside. A friend from Writers' Project days pretended not to see Phil when they passed on Madison Avenue. A Westchester neighbor who was climbing the corporate ladder in a Fortune 500 company sheepishly brought us his copy of "The Paris Commune" by Karl Marx. He had thrown away the rest of his left wing library but could not bear to destroy this pamphlet, which was the first English-language edition of the manifesto of the International Workingmen's Association in 1870. He promised to reclaim it when it would once again be expedient to put it on his bookshelf. I still have the pamphlet.

We no longer marched on May Day shouting "DEFEND THE SOVIET UNION." Knowledge of the purges and labor camps lay in the future, but I had developed serious doubts about communism, Russian style. I had begun to read biology texts in order to write children's books about plants and insects and was immediately disturbed by the rise of Trofim Lysenko, Stalin's protégé, who rejected western genetics and declared that acquired characteristics could be inherited. In addition to claiming that he had "vernalized" winter wheat to produce earlier harvests, he demonstrated a "potomato" whose roots bore potatoes and its branches, tomatoes. I dreamed of Lysenko tiptoeing through his garden at night tying tomatoes to potato plants in the manner of the old song, "When apples grew on the lilac bush." After Julian Huxley and J. B. S. Haldane, British Marxist scientists, declared that Lysenko was a charlatan whose theories had resulted in lower crop yields, I concluded that science could not flourish under a dictatorship.

Far more bone-chilling than Lysenko's ideas were the indications of Soviet anti-Semitism. At first we dismissed these as Cold War propaganda. Hadn't the Soviet Union been the first country to abolish racial discrimination? Its policy on national minorities was embedded in its constitution. There was even a Jewish Autonomous Region, Birobidzhan, which we had read about before the war. But the U.S. press was reprinting caricatures from *krokodil*, the Soviet humor magazine, which resembled the illustrations in Nazi publications. Then Stalin announced the "Doctors' Plot," a bizarre tale of doctors, most of them Jewish, who had murdered high government officials and planned to kill Stalin. Before the doctors were brought to trial Stalin died. During the next days, as we read the *New York Times'* reports of the grim power struggle in Red Square, I lost my last lingering faith in the dictatorship of the proletariat.

On the night of Stalin's death, Phil met Jack Ryan, former president of the New York Newspaper Guild, in the Ritz Men's Bar (no women allowed). After a few drinks, the sentimental Irishman and the sentimental Jew wept, not for Stalin but for the death of their youthful dreams.

Disillusioned by the Soviet Union, I was not happy in my Westchester Party branch either. The main business of our meetings was fundraising — to support the Communist leaders who were on trial for conspiracy. This meant Saturday night parties. Endless boring hours were spent deciding who would make which canapés, bring the liquor, and "give the pitch"; that is, make the speech asking for donations. The parties were scarcely distinguishable from other Westchester affairs where people danced, flirted, and drank too much. Since I did not dance or flirt and had only a limited capacity for alcohol, I finally stopped attending meetings. I stayed out of the Party for a year, until Rose, county organizer of the Party, came to me with a proposition. She had stayed with us for weeks at a time, babysitting when the children were younger and becoming a part of our family circle. She told me of a new branch whose members were to devote themselves to fighting McCarthyism. Instead of following Party directives they were to work on their own, devising ways of changing public opinion. To avoid being labeled Reds, they were to stay away from all Party meetings, including those Saturday night fundraisers that I disliked.

I joined the Rye Democratic Party and the League of Women Voters, talking politics whenever the opportunity arose. My neighbor Jeanne Webber, a former *Fortune* researcher who was not a Party member, worked with me to initiate informal gatherings of local liberals who wanted to discuss the rise of Senator Joseph McCarthy. David Dempsey, a Rye resident who reviewed books for the *New York Times*, reported on repression in the publishing industry; and a lawyer from Port Chester telephoned to ask to be invited "to your interesting discussions." Thirty-five-year-old William Kunstler, later a fiery civil rights lawyer who defended Martin Luther King, Jr. and the Chicago Seven, was then practicing conventional law in New York, in partnership with his brother. Because he "always needed a lot of stimulation," he said, he had started a radio program on WMCA, New York's municipal station, where he interviewed people as diverse as Eleanor Roosevelt and Malcolm X. When he and his wife, Lotte, invited Phil and me to dinner, their other guest was Langston Hughes, the black writer. At a subsequent meeting of our anti-McCarthy group, Hughes traveled from New York to tell us of his appearance before McCarthy's subcommittee. Bill

Kunstler also joined Jeanne and me in writing letters to the Port Chester *Daily Item*, lambasting their right-wing editorials and scolding the local VFW post, whose members had volunteered to investigate local subversives and report them to the FBI. As people in other Westchester towns also organized, by June 1954 we had sufficient money and signatures for full-page advertisements in the local papers, which said, "McCarthy practiced calculated fraud and deceit on the United States Senate and on the people of the United States."

McCarthy's downfall, which came soon afterward, did not mean the end of the persecution of communists. With so many leaders on trial or in prison, the Party believed that fascism was imminent and that the best hope of survival was to go underground. Some one hundred or so lower echelon leaders were designated "operative but unavailable." They left their families, assumed new identities, and were prepared to take over the Party if the worst happened. Our friend Rose became an "unavailable." Attached to the Southern Regional Committee, she traveled from the South to New York, arranging meetings and keeping committee members in touch with one another. She stayed with us when in the neighborhood, arriving late at night and leaving early the next day. Although the new Communist Control Act contained penalties for anyone convicted of "harboring a fugitive" we did not hesitate to offer her bed and breakfast and the use of our washing machine. Technically we were doing nothing illegal; no warrant had been issued for her arrest. Besides, we believed the Act unconstitutional, although the Supreme Court did not so rule until 1965.

Nor did we think twice when she asked us to shelter members of her committee for brief stays. She arrived one night with Junius Scales, Party leader of four southern states. Thirty-two-year-old Junius, a member of a distinguished North Carolina family (his grandfather had been governor), was a warm, friendly man who charmed Peter and Anne by his interest in their lives, talked politics with Phil and black history with me. On one of his visits, he brought me a copy of Charles Dickens's *American Notes*, a book that I referred to often in later writing. He was a model house guest who not only made his bed and washed dishes but taught me a foolproof method of frying eggs. If he was an example of what communist leaders were like, I gave them high marks.

Thus we were saddened when, in November 1954, newspapers carried photographs of Junius Scales in handcuffs, on his way to stand trial in North Carolina for advocating the violent overthrow of the government. His 1955 conviction reversed by the Supreme Court, this gentle, sensitive man was tried again in 1958, after he had left the Party, and sentenced to six years in prison, the longest term given to any

Communist. He served fifteen months in Lewisburg Penitentiary before President John F. Kennedy, in a changed atmosphere, pardoned him.

Our other visit from an "unavailable" was more like a spy movie. Because he was black, Edward Strong, head of the Southern Regional Committee, would have been conspicuous if glimpsed through our floor-to-ceiling windows. Rose smuggled him into the house after dark and installed him in the guest room with the drapes tightly pulled. For several tense days I brought him his meals on a tray while the children discouraged their friends from visiting. Although I was relieved when Rose picked him up, I had been surprisingly calm during his visit. Not only did I believe that the Red Hunt was unjust, but I felt somehow invulnerable. Surely the government could not punish me for exercising rights guaranteed by the Constitution.*

Occasionally there were chinks in this armor of invulnerability. The Internal Security Act called for the possible detention of Communist Party members. After we read that the FBI was refurbishing the camps in which the Japanese had been interned during the war, several couples met in our living room for a painful decision. Should we ask sisters and brothers to take our children if we were detained, or should we

---

*Edward Strong was arrested in 1956 but died of leukemia before he could be brought to trial.

bring them with us to the detention camp? Solemnly we decided to keep our children with us. Fortunately, we were not called on to implement this decision.

There were other penalties for our rash behavior, however. Kirby Lane North became known as "Red Hill," in part because our neighbor, Goodwin Watson, a distinguished professor at Teachers College, was denounced as a Red by the American Legion. Although Goodwin answered their charges, there were whispers all over town. "You can tell they're communists," the man who delivered our *New York Times* told a friend. "They never hang up a wreath at Christmas." I had difficulty hiring a plumber or electrician and felt that clerks in some Main Street stores waited on me reluctantly.

The Rye post office opened our mail. Letters arrived days late with envelopes clumsily resealed. We were not being paranoid about this. A friend of Peter's, who was close to the postmaster's son, confirmed that we were on a special list. The Webbers' mail was opened, too, and so was Alice's, although she had had no contact with the Party since college. I wondered what happened to the thousands of letters that Rye and Harrison postal clerks read. They had no copying machines in those days, so probably they microfilmed our correspondence. Perhaps, in a third sub-basement of the FBI building, there are still reels of microfilm containing Mother's letters to Alice and me.

We were disturbed when our insurance agent phoned to tell us that Allstate Insurance had canceled our homeowner's policy because they feared they would be vulnerable to loss under the "riot and civil commotion" clause. Whether we would riot or indignant citizens would rise against us was not clear. Happily, the insurance agent, a fellow member of the American Labor Party, was able to obtain insurance for us with another, possibly less well-informed, company.

The penalties Phil faced at CBS were more severe. By the 1950s hiring of performers in radio and television was controlled by the self-appointed censors who published *Red Channels* and *Counterattack*. If these publications declared that an actor or writer had communist affiliations, he was blacklisted. Phil escaped their notice because he worked in CBS's publicity department, where his name did not come before the public. His boss, who had a shrewd idea of Phil's politics, hinted that if he worked long hours uncomplainingly and never, never asked for a raise, he would not be brought to the attention of the vice-president in charge of blacklisting. Phil turned out reams of press releases on radio performers, and worked nights and weekends writing CBS's annual report as well as speeches for company executives to deliver.

Hard work, however, could not shield him from bad luck. One morning, a young actor also named Philip Sterling who was appearing in CBS soap operas telephoned to ask Phil to meet him in the coffee shop of the CBS building. Phil went downstairs sensing trouble. The actor had just been blacklisted and denied all acting assignments because, said *Counterattack*, he had autographed a book by Earl Browder in 1938.

Phil remembered the incident. During his Writers' Project days, the Party unit had given a farewell party and a copy of Browder's *The People's Front* to Edwin Banta, an aging comrade who was retiring. Banta asked everyone to autograph the book. Phil disliked Banta, but when the book was presented to him, he wrote, "Anything the others say goes for me." The others—106 of them—had written such phrases as "Revolutionary greetings" and "Yours for a Soviet America." Later Banta had inserted a sentence above the signatures, saying that the book had been presented to him by members of the Federal Writers' Project Party unit "in recognition of his untiring efforts in behalf of our Party and Communism." Then he had turned the book over to the House Un-American Activities Committee. Banta's appearance as a witness had given the committee an opportunity to declare that the Writers' Project was communist-controlled. The names of the 106 people who had signed his book remained in HUAC's files; now, more than fifteen years later, they were in the hands of *Counterattack*.

Over coffee, Phil pointed out to the young actor that since he had only been in his teens when the

Browder book was autographed, he should be able to convince *Counterattack* that he was not the signator. If *Counterattack* refused to remove him from the blacklist, then Phil promised to come forward, although, he noted soberly, "It will cost me my job." A decent man, young Philip Sterling cleared his name and returned to acting while Phil continued at Press Information.

His problems were not over. Twice FBI men stopped him in the lobby of the CBS building when he was leaving for the day. Flashing his identification, one said, "We want to talk to you about your communist past." Phil replied, as we had been advised to do, "I have nothing to say," and brushed past them. They did not pursue him.

The FBI also turned up in Rye. One afternoon Devera Ehrenberg came over to report that there was a car parked at the end of the road. Two men wearing trenchcoats and snap-brimmed hats—the standard FBI attire—had come to the Ehrenbergs' door and asked for her father. Mike had fought in the Spanish Civil War, and all veterans of the Abraham Lincoln Brigade were being interrogated. Warned by phone, Mike took an assignment on the West Coast, staying away from home until the FBI men lost patience and departed.

The children, who had been told not to let trenchcoated strangers into the house, enjoyed the drama, as they had when Junius Scales and Ed Strong stayed with us. We refrained from telling them that we were Party members because we did not want them burdened with the information if they were questioned, but we made a point of introducing them to important figures on the left who had been blacklisted. W. E. B. Du Bois was the most illustrious black man in the United States until he accepted the chairmanship of the Peace Information Center, which was allied to the international peace movement and circulated petitions calling for the abolition of atomic war. Du Bois and his associates were indicted as agents of a foreign power. Although the case against them was eventually dismissed, Du Bois was denied a passport and persecuted in a number of ways. For several years admirers gave birthday parties in his honor, but the affairs were held in Harlem or on the Upper West Side because downtown hotels refused space for "Commie gatherings." We attended the earlier birthdays, and when it came time for his 90th we brought Peter and Anne with us. At the Roosevelt Hotel on 44th Street—the Cold War was losing momentum—we all heard Du Bois address his two-month-old great-grandson. He advised him to find work that he wanted to do and that was socially useful.

In the same spring of 1958 Peter, Jeanne Webber, and I made weekly trips to New York for a course in black history that Du Bois was teaching. He had been teaching at the left-wing Jefferson School until the government closed it down. Our course was in a loft building on lower Fifth Avenue. Some twenty students, mostly middle-aged and white, sat on folding chairs while Du Bois, still an erect figure, with a dry New England accent, lectured on the glories that were Africa and the horrors of slavery in the United States. We felt privileged to hear this man who had written his first book on black history in 1896, but it was sad to realize that he could find no broader rostrum. Anne was too young for the Du Bois course, but one snowy Sunday afternoon I drove her to Harlem to hear Paul Robeson. Turned away at most concert halls in the United States, and unable to travel abroad because the State Department refused to give him a passport, Robeson gave magnificent concerts at his brother's A. M. E. Zion Church on West 136th Street.

Our dinner table at night was a noisy affair, as each reported on the events of the day. Not all of the discussions were political. In elementary school, Peter had been paired in the Christmas pageant with a girl who had cerebral palsy. Fearing that he would look like a fool, he was determined to refuse the part until Phil, who was our conscience, convinced him that he must go through with it because it was the right thing to do. In high school, when he was in charge of the monitors in the lunchroom, he complained that one of the few black boys in the school picked fights and was disruptive. Peter planned to report him to the principal; Phil proposed that he appoint the boy a monitor instead. I thought this was too much to ask of Peter, but Phil prevailed and the boy's behavior improved dramatically.

In school, the Kirby Lane North children were initially perceived as different because they lived in modern houses in a community where colonial architecture was the norm, and because their parents were photographers, professors, and writers rather than Madison Avenue executives. As they grew older and made friends in school, Peter had an easier time than Anne. Boys were allowed to be different, but in the 1950s, girls were expected to conform. I had exacerbated Anne's problems by telling her that she was capable of learning science and math. But when she spoke out in class, she was ostracized.

Anne was far from the only youngster with radical parents who had a hard time in Westchester schools in the 1950s. Some red diaper babies were roughed up by youthful Red hunters. We joined with parents in other communities to help the young people form a Saturday morning discussion group. Meeting in Rye or Croton-on-Hudson, a center for radicals since the days of John Reed, they discussed politics and their personal problems and read pamphlets on political economy under the guidance of a genial Marxist scholar. Peter and Anne attended the Saturday morning group until they went off to college — long after Phil and I had left the Communist Party.

On June 5, 1956, the *New York Times* published the text of a speech delivered by Nikita Khrushchev at the 20th Congress of the Soviet Party. Everything that the enemies of the Soviet Union had charged was true, from the trials of the 1930s to the Doctors' Plot almost twenty years later: torture, imprisonment in labor camps, the slaughter of tens of thousands, and the "cult of the personality" that had enabled Stalin to carry out these atrocities. When my branch met that night, people were stunned, angry, incredulous. "I have been living a lie," the chairman said.

We did not need to resign from the communist Party. It dissolved around us. The county organizer returned to his vocation as a music teacher. The literature agent retrieved the stack of pamphlets he had stored in our deep closet and dumped them in Long Island Sound. No more meetings were scheduled. Even among close friends there were few discussions. The Party continued to function in New York and other places where revisionists fought diehards and sought to save some shreds of the organization, but Phil and I never had any contact with it again.

We were sad and ashamed of our gullibility, but we did not feel that we had been "living a lie." The Party had given us goals, a sense of purpose that transcended our daily lives. And at the time of Khrushchev's terrible revelations, we were already involved in another struggle, the fight of black Americans to achieve equality.

CHAPTER

11

In the dark days of the McCarthy period there was one bright spot on the political horizon. On May 17, 1954, Supreme Court justices asked a momentous question: "Does segregation of children in public school solely on the basis of race deprive the children of the minority group of equal educational opportunities?" Unanimously the justices replied, "We believe that it does. To separate them solely because of their race generates a feeling of inferiority that may affect their hearts and minds in a way unlikely ever to be undone. Separate educational facilities are inherently unequal."

Along with most of my generation, I had accepted the dictum of humorist Finley Peter Dunne: "The Supreme Court follows the election returns." But now a conservative court had handed down the most significant decision in American history, one that could destroy the whole ugly tangle of Jim Crow and put the nation on the road to equality. At a meeting of the Port Chester-Rye branch of the National Association for the Advancement of Colored People, Phil and I joined in the cheering.

We had been members of the branch since our first years in Rye. We lived little more than a mile from a row of dilapidated tenements in Port Chester, the neighboring industrial community. Once or twice a year, usually on a cold winter night, we would be awakened by the wail of fire sirens and would know that there had been yet another disastrous fire on South Main Street. For a few days people of good will would turn out to distribute food and clothing to the homeless while the NAACP and black churches tried to find them shelter—a difficult task, since both Port Chester and Rye neighborhoods were segregated. Phil joined NAACP branch chairman Robert Brown, a soft-spoken, humorous man who was a postman by day, in calling on the owner of the tenements to ask him to repair flagrant violations of the building code. He turned out to be a genuine slumlord, so evil that he could have stepped out of the pages of a proletarian novel. Not only did he blame the fires on his tenants' carelessness and refuse to make repairs, but he later headed a veterans group that was bent on ferreting out local Reds.

Although a few other white people were nominal members of the NAACP, we were the only ones who regularly attended the monthly meetings and took part in the work. Chairman of the housing committee, Phil also helped with fundraising. I spoke on Harriet Tubman during Negro History Week and brought

Peter and Anne along for special occasions, including the Fourth of July picnic, where Phil won the hearts of the women by making potato salad—the only man in the branch who cooked for the day.

We were not doing this because of any Party directive—after 1956 we did not follow Party directives—but because knowing our black neighbors enriched our lives. And we certainly were made to feel more welcome in the Bethesda Baptist Church, where branch meetings were held, than in one of the prosperous Protestant congregations in Rye.

I was reading widely in black history, planning additional books, while Phil convinced his boss that CBS should send press releases to the *Amsterdam News* and the *Pittsburgh Courier* as he did to the radio and television columnists on the *Times* and *Daily News*. Before long he was buying lunches for James Hicks, executive editor of the *Amsterdam News*, Alan Morrison, *Ebony*'s New York editor, and Evelyn Cunningham of the *Courier*, and inviting them and their families for summer Sundays in Rye. After talking politics and children, we soon felt comfortable enough with each other to discuss the situation of black people in the United States. We listened enthralled as they told not only of Harlem today but also tales from slavery, when black people used "upside-down-the-wall" talk to conceal their thoughts from "Mr. Charlie" and "Miss Ann."

Because of his CBS ties Phil was able to bring Broadway and Harlem performers to Port Chester. In the 1950s he brought the cast of *Take a Giant Step*, one of the first black-written plays on Broadway, to perform scenes from the play. The Sterling family had the pleasure of meeting the cast at the train station and serving them supper after the play—and Anne promptly developed a crush on 17-year-old Louis Gossett, who played the leading role.

Probably Phil's greatest triumph as an impresario was the night he brought Jackie "Moms" Mabley, the legendary comedienne, to a boarded-up theater in Port Chester. Caught between the demise of vaudeville and the rise of television, Moms Mabley was glad to perform a one-night stand for the benefit of the NAACP. Every seat in the theater on North Main Street was filled, as whites as well as blacks came from all over Westchester. Shortly after her appearance for us, she made a comeback not only at the Apollo in Harlem but at the Kennedy White House.

These encounters only increased my interest in writing another black biography. While I searched for a subject, I continued to work on photographic books with Mike Ehrenberg. At Peggy Lesser's request, we produced *Wall Street: The Story of the Stock Exchange* and *Polio Pioneers*, the latter published when millions of children received their first shots of polio vaccine. In addition to these, we did two nature books, *Insects and the*

Close to My Heart

Homes They Build and *The Story of Mosses, Ferns and Mushrooms*. There were so few science books for young readers in 1955 that the latter became Mike's and my best-seller, doing well when it was first issued and even better after the Russians launched *Sputnik* and energized the study of science in U.S. schools.

Doubleday salesmen were less enthusiastic about my next project, a biography of Robert Smalls, a slave who stole the *Planter*, a Confederate gunboat, sailed it past the guns of Fort Sumter, and turned it over to the Union fleet. The first black Civil War hero, Smalls became a U.S. congressman during Reconstruction and continued as a leader of South Carolina until his death in 1915. Despite his remarkable career, no one had written a full-length biography of him.

I pursued him at the Schomburg Collection, where typescript reminiscences led me to his son, William Robert Smalls, head of the Urban League in Warren, Ohio. Willie Smalls and his wife made two trips to Rye to tell me all that he could recall about his father, and to give me introductions to family friends in his home town of Beaufort, South Carolina. The National Archives sent me the official army and navy reports on Smalls' exploit; the *Congressional Record* yielded some speeches, and during a trip to Washington I located letters at the Library of Congress and at Howard University. The high point of this trip was meeting Dorothy Porter, curator of the Moorland-Spingarn

Collection at Howard University. Dorothy, who had earned a master's degree in library science at Columbia in 1932, had built the collection of books and manuscripts at Howard into one of the world's richest repositories of black history and culture. An enthusiast as well as a scholar, she would go through her files and always turn up something new for me to read. At the end of the day she brought me home to meet her husband, James Porter, a Howard professor and artist. When I marveled at the elegant dinner she turned out in no time, she showed me her secret, a freezer stocked with steaks and gourmet sauces. For many years she had served as a hostess for the State Department, entertaining African dignitaries who were turned away from hotels and restaurants in the nation's segregated capitol. Although a Supreme Court decision two years earlier now required the hostelries to open their doors to all, Dorothy and Jimmy continued to serve perfect martinis and special dinners. We also found that we shared a fascination for research in all aspects of African-American history. By mail, phone, and occasional visits over the next forty years, we became good friends.

After I had put together the basic outlines of Smalls's life, Phil used part of his vacation to accompany me to Beaufort. We set out by car in September 1955, the second September after the Supreme Court's decision on segregation. In the District of Columbia and in border states schools were beginning to obey the court order, but in the deep South, White Citizens Councils called for massive resistance. Crossing the Mason-Dixon line for the first time, we behaved like typical tourists. We stopped to marvel at our first sight of a cotton field and dined at roadside barbecues, those tasty predecessors of fast-food stands.

Beaufort, on one of the Sea Islands, was a picturesque old town, its quiet streets lined with palmettos and live oaks dripping with Spanish moss. We stayed at the Golden Eagle Inn, a hostelry that embodied all that we had read about southern hospitality. When we requested a wakeup call, we were awakened by a white-coated youngster bringing a silver coffee service. Breakfasts of country ham and grits sustained our mood. From the inn I walked to the public library to read microfilm copies of black newspapers from the Reconstruction period that had not been available in Washington or New York.

At first glance, everything in Beaufort spelled peace and harmony. Only when we called on the people William Smalls had given us introductions to did we discover two Beauforts, one white, one black. Black Beaufort also dispensed hospitality. We were invited to lunch and tea and, one memorable evening, to see a night-blooming cereus in flower. The older people recalled Robert Smalls in his late years, a portly figure who spoke in their school assembly, telling about the

Civil War and the value of a good education. Their younger relatives explained, with humor and some bitterness, the facts of segregation. They had never been inside the Golden Eagle Inn; no restaurant in town would sell them a cup of coffee. They avoided the movies because going there meant climbing outside stairs to the Jim Crow balcony; they stayed off the buses rather than ride in the rear. The principal of the black elementary school was hurt to learn from me that the library had a microfilm reader; she had never been inside the building, although as a special acknowledgment of her position she was allowed to borrow books at the rear door. The black librarian begged us to call at her building, where half-empty shelves contained the tattered discards from the white library.

We visited the segregated Robert Smalls High School at the edge of town, the cemetery where Smalls was buried, and his old home, owned by a white couple from the North who permitted us to tour the house and grounds. A young newspaperman took us by bateau — the broad-bottomed boat that had once been the means of transport between the Sea Islands — to an island where only black families lived and children ran away at the sight of our white faces.

For a week we went back and forth, crossing the line that divided Beaufort's two worlds. The handful of elderly white people who knew Robert Smalls when he had been the town's most prominent citizen refused to talk with me, insisting angrily, fearfully, that they were too busy or were leaving town. But when we returned to the inn at night for splendid dinners of crab cakes or shrimp, guests and innkeeper alike could scarcely conceal their curiosity. We had been seen entering the handsome antebellum homes that freedmen had purchased at the end of the Civil War. "What are the houses like inside?" asked a woman who had lived in Beaufort all her life. "And what were you doing there?" a stringer for the Associated Press bluntly inquired. Even before the *Beaufort Gazette* blew our cover with a paragraph about my book under the heading "News of Particular Interest to the Colored Community," the waiters in the dining room, most of them high school students who had seen us at the Robert Smalls School, crowded around our table, eager to talk. They knew all about the Supreme Court's decision. When did we think it would be implemented? Next year? The year after? They were full of confidence about the future.

We traveled home by way of Charleston, less exuberant than when we had started. The husband of the school principal, a funeral director, had mentioned driving thirty-six hours at a stretch to pick up deceased Harlemites who had wanted to be buried back home. When I asked why he drove so long without stopping, he looked at me as if in pity for my ignorance. "Because there is no place where I can eat or sleep along the way," he replied. We were conscious of our white skin privilege when we booked into a motel on the outskirts of Charleston. Motels were just beginning to supplant the tourist homes we usually stayed in, and this one was luxurious, with wall-to-wall carpeting, a good shower, and even a kidney-shaped swimming pool. For whites only. There was no need for a sign. Everyone in South Carolina knew.

Back at my desk, I realized that although I had started out with an adventure tale in which the hero battled odds to final victory, I had a more complicated story to tell. For a half-century Robert Smalls had been present at every significant historical event in South Carolina. A wartime hero and a political leader during Reconstruction, he had represented his district in Congress and had fought vainly at the 1895 state constitutional convention, which disenfranchised blacks and ushered in the crazy quilt of Jim Crow that still blocked black people's chance for full lives.

Captain of the Planter was a difficult book to write for a junior high audience as I found my emphasis shifting from the Civil War to the first heady years of freedom, followed by the nation's cynical betrayal of its promises. I based my interpretation of Reconstruction on the lives of Smalls and his contemporaries, but it differed so widely from the then conventional depiction of the "tragic era" that I anticipated trouble when Doubleday editors read the manuscript. I was not surprised, therefore, when Peggy Lesser's first comment on *Captain of the Planter* was, "Dear, you sound as if you hate white people."

Fortunately, she was fair-minded enough to submit the book to leading black librarians, Arna Bontemps at Fisk University and Augusta Baker at the New York Public Library, who supported my interpretation of history and recommended publication. *Captain of the Planter: The Story of Robert Smalls*, with illustrations by Ernest Crichlow, was published in January 1958. Reviews were favorable, except for a snide one in the Charleston *News and Courier*, but the book never sold well, probably because I had tried to cram in too much history for young readers.

By September 1956, the third September after the Supreme Court decision, heckling crowds surrounded the schools in the mid-South. In newspapers and on television we saw men and women screaming, "Go home, nigger!", throwing rocks, and even spitting at black children. The contrast between the hate-filled white faces and the quiet eyes-front demeanor of the black youngsters was infinitely moving. So were the interviews with the children who told reporters, "I'm not going to school to socialize. I just want an education."

I was rewriting the Smalls biography and completing another nature book, but I felt that I had to get involved with this "children's crusade," which held the key to the future of race relations in the United States. However, when I proposed that Mike and I go South to document the battle of these black youngsters, Peggy Lesser turned me down. There were sound business reasons for her rejection. All over the South, White Citizens Councils and the Ku Klux Klan were organizing reprisals not only against blacks who dared to cross the color line but against businesses that expressed sympathy for them. Already there were boycotts of Ford cars and Philip Morris cigarettes, because both companies had contributed to organizations like the Urban League. Thus Doubleday might face a South-wide boycott against all of its books if it published one that sympathized with black children.

Arthur Wang and Larry Hill, acquaintances of ours, had recently founded a small, liberal-oriented publishing house. With less to lose than Doubleday, they gave Mike and me a contract and a small advance to visit recently desegregated schools in Kentucky, Tennessee, Delaware, and Virginia. We started out in April 1957, armed with introductions from the NAACP and Southern Regional Council. Our first stop was Louisville, Kentucky, whose schools had been integrated the previous fall. There a high school senior told us of opening day, when she ran a gauntlet of hostile people: "I went marching up the steps that first morning, my head up like I was sniffing pies in heaven.

I felt like I was an ambassador from some foreign country." Did white children talk like this? I didn't think so. Our next call was Fort Knox, where the government-run schools had integrated without difficulty. In the kindergarten, Mike took a photograph of a black child hugging a white doll, a picture so moving that after we had used it on the cover of our book, it was widely reprinted; it still turns up today, without credit to the photographer.

In the coal-mining towns of western Kentucky, where integration had been halted by threatening mobs, we heard of black Louise Gordon, who had brought her children to Clay's white school for eleven days, and Margaret Meazles, mother of the only white youngsters who attended school with the Gordons. Louise Gordon was gone, driven across the state line to Indiana after months of persecution. With the help of a sympathetic minister—who soon was transferred to a parish in Utah—I interviewed her by mail.

Her son James had heard about black children going to white schools and asked why he and his sister couldn't go to the school in Clay. "I told him, 'If you've got the guts to go, I've got the guts to take you.' After the first day with the crowds screaming and all I lost my nerve. I asked them if they wanted to go back and they said, Yes. I couldn't take their courage from them, so I would let them go and die a thousand deaths until three o'clock."

"Mrs. Meazles seems to be a very wonderful woman," she continued. We thought so too, although we had a hard time finding her. She was a native of Clay, but no one on its main street would admit to knowing her. When I inquired in the post office, the clerk at the window snarled, "She ain't no patron of mine" and angrily turned his back on further inquiries. We drove along a winding mountain road outside of town, uneasily aware that reporters' cars had been rammed there during the early days of the integration struggle. At last a gas station attendant took pity on us and directed us to Mrs. Meazles. A miner's wife, she had brought her children to school during the white boycott simply because she thought it was right. "To me they're just people," she said.

In Corydon, Kentucky, we visited a Negro school that lacked a gymnasium, lunchroom, and indoor plumbing; only five hundred yards away stood a white school, a new brick building with all the amenities. In Sturgis, where the black children had already been sent back to the colored school, Margaret, the daughter of a coal miner, told us, "I felt okay going to Sturgis High. We live here and I felt as if I was entitled to go. But when all those people yelled things I would get kinda shaky. My science class, that was the best class I would like to go to. At the colored school we don't have any science." In Morganfield, Jonathan described his prospects: "I want to be an engineer, but when I talked to the people at the colleges, they said I would qualify better for physical education. I have just two years of math, no physics, no chemistry, no languages. We had French until the board of education heard about it. They said no need of French for the Negroes."

From Kentucky we drove to Oak Ridge and Clinton, Tennessee. Oak Ridge, a town under jurisdiction of the Atomic Energy Commisssion, had easily desegregated, but the neighboring town of Clinton had been in crisis since September, when fifteen black children enrolled in its high school. Jeering mobs had been followed by beatings, tire slashings, midnight telephone threats, and finally a bomb that damaged thirty Negro homes and injured two people. By the time we arrived the number of Negro students had been whittled down to eight, but on the surface the town was quiet.

"But I still wouldn't drive there in your car with New York license plates," the chairman of Oak Ridge's Community Relations Council advised.

"Nobody'll bother us," we protested.

"Maybe not, but nobody'll dare talk to you if you park your Yankee car in front of their house."

That's how it happened that his children went to Sunday School in Mike's sporty convertible while we drove to Clinton in a sedate sedan with Tennessee plates. Introduced to the leaders of the Negro community, we were looked over carefully before we were allowed to talk with the high school students, including

Bobby Cain, "the one that was mobbed." The youngsters spoke cautiously—"It's pretty good, better than it
used to be. Some will speak to you"—then, recalling
indignities, with more heat: "They poured ink in our
lockers. In the hall they step on our heels. Mornings
they stand out in front of school, calling things as we
come in. In study hall they kick the backs of our chairs.
We decided not to carry knives, not even jackknives,
because the first thing they jostle you and then they
yell, 'He's got a knife.' We all agreed not to go out for
baseball or basketball, 'cause of all the trouble."

After eight months of integration they still found it
safer to go to school together. We walked with them
the next morning, Mike snapping pictures while I tried
to stay out of camera range. Tight-lipped and strained,
looking neither right nor left, they trudged along,
trying to ignore the muttered epithets. We spent the
morning in Clinton High School, talking to teachers
and students. Although some recognized what a difficult time the black students were having, I was disappointed to find that no one dared reach out a hand in
sympathy. Close to tears when we left, I was slightly
consoled a month later when newspapers carried a picture of Bobby Cain in cap and gown, a member of his
graduating class. Black children returned the next
year, but in the fall of 1958 three dynamite blasts
destroyed the school.

Close to My Heart

From Clinton we drove to Rock Hill, South Carolina, to visit St. Anne's parochial school, the only integrated school in the state. The detour was worthwhile because of our meeting with Hester Claxton, a remarkable twelve-year-old, who "did a lot of thinking" before she told her parish priest that she would leave her neighborhood school and travel across town to St. Anne's, where she knew that she would encounter hostility. "It's because they don't know me well enough," she explained. "Many white people hold fear against the colored. By me coming to this school it might help others to understand."

Traveling north to cities in Virginia, Delaware, and Maryland, where integration had been accomplished relatively peacefully, we heard the now familiar sentiments: "The grown people think we're going to school to socialize, but that's not my goal. I think all children should have the same opportunities. Besides, I wanted to show that I could do the same work they did. And I can." I arrived home tired, having spent every evening in my motel room typing up my notes to make sure that I had not missed a word, but I felt uplifted by the children's courage and clear-sightedness. I believed that I had more than a story to tell to young people. I wanted to bring about change. I wanted to make people of good will understand the rightness of the children's crusade and the three hundred years of injustice that underlay it.

But two weeks in the South, all we had been able to spend, was not enough for an in-depth sociological study. The subject needed a cry from the heart, the kind of eloquence that was beginning to be heard from Martin Luther King, Jr., but I could not match his style. Besides, I was writing as a white woman. Despite the depth of my feelings, I was not sure if I could express the same emotions as a black person would. After weeks of false starts I settled for a first-person account of the trip, with extensive quotations from the children and their parents and, of course, Mike's moving photographs.

By the time that *Tender Warriors* reached the office of Hill and Wang, the nation was experiencing another of its autumnal outbreaks, one even more violent than the year before. While armed mobs and dynamite blasts threatened black people all over the South, the spotlight focused on Little Rock, Arkansas, where nine black children were entering Central High School. Throughout the school year, the black teenagers attended high school while soldiers patrolled the school corridors. I brought *Tender Warriors* up to date with four pages on Little Rock, concluding with excerpts from a radio discussion in which white and black students talked together for the first time.

Published in the spring of 1958, *Tender Warriors* was the first eyewitness account of school desegregation. Although *Ebony* used a five-page spread from the book and Roy Wilkins of the NAACP wrote a glowing blurb, reviews were scarce and sales underwhelming. One small perk then available to publishers was the export of books to the 250 overseas libraries operated by the United States Information Service. Several years earlier, two McCarthy minions had investigated these libraries, and found that the collections included mystery stories by radical Dashiel Hammett, historical fiction by former communist Howard Fast, and poetry by Langston Hughes, who had once expressed sympathy for the Soviet Union. Although McCarthy was now dead and dishonored, USIS had not forgotten the inquisition. Even before *Tender Warriors* was published, Hill and Wang were informed that the book was "disallowed" for shipment abroad. Despite Larry Hill's letters of protest, the USIS clearance officer continued to maintain that the book was "not eligible for export." USIS libraries were intended to show the United States at its best, and *Tender Warriors* pointed to an unfortunate flaw in American democracy. However, the Liberty Book Club, founded by blacklisted editors, chose the book as its spring selection, and the edition of 5,000 copies was sold out.

Tender Warriors was never reprinted, but I could not forget those children. I had had an extraordinary experience, and I still wanted to grab people and say, "This is what is going on. These are the heroes we should be celebrating." Finally a friend, perhaps weary of listening to me, suggested that I write a fictional account of a black child's first year in a desegregated school. When I told Peggy Lesser about it, her response was, "Set it in the North." In northern cities, including nearby New Rochelle, black parents were protesting *de facto* segregation, schools that were segregated because neighborhoods were, rather than because of a law. True, black children met hostility in New Rochelle, but they never faced screaming mobs; after school they could buy a soda on Main Street or shop at Macy's without being snubbed. The story I was bursting to tell had to be set in the segregated South. Peggy Lesser at last gave in, but the contract she sent differed from those I had previously signed. Typed into the printed form was a clause saying, "In the event that a complete satisfactory manuscript is not received," the advance would be repaid from my other royalties.

Although this was hardly a vote of confidence, I went ahead with a story about twelve-year-old Mary Jane Douglas, who lived in a mid-South city and was one of two black youngsters entering an all-white junior high school under court order. Borrowing freely from the experiences of the children I had talked with in the South, and even black teenagers in Rye, I followed Mary Jane through the school year as she was threatened, harassed, and condescended to. When she finally made a friend, they discovered that there was no place they could meet after school because the park had a WHITES ONLY sign; the drugstore refused to serve Mary Jane, and neither set of parents encouraged home visits. Finishing the story was a problem. Happy endings were virtually compulsory in juvenile novels, but I did not want to mislead readers by telling them that Mary Jane could live happily ever after she survived a year in an integrated school. I compromised by having the two girls join the science club, where they found limited acceptance and some hope that things would be better next year.

Ordinarily a slow writer, I was so moved by the story I had to tell that I wrote at top speed, wrapping my legs tightly around the typewriter table until they ached when I uncurled them at the end of the day. I interrupted the book once to accompany Phil to North Carolina. While I had been reading microfilm in the Beaufort library, he had been collecting jokes and stories for a long-planned anthology of black humor and folklore. A Beaufort acquaintance told him to get in touch with Carol Bowie, who knew more stories than anyone else in the country. Carol was a psychologist with a Ph.D. from the University of Chicago, but she was teaching at segregated North Carolina College in Durham and living in rural Henderson, some forty miles outside the city. When Phil wrote her about his project, she immediately invited us to visit her.

"You're not going to stay with a strange colored woman!" my mother expostulated. Strange indeed.

Carol's square-built frame house would not have been out of place on any Westchester street, and her notion of hospitality was to fill her guest bedroom with flowers and a box of chocolates, and to serve a steak dinner. Afterwards, her neighbors dropped in to tell Phil stories. The next day she took us to North Carolina College, where there was a folklorist Phil wanted to meet. While he tape-recorded stories, the school administrator gleefully explained to me how she got her budget approved by the state legislature. Since the legislators were not interested in improving black students' intellects, she asked them to appropriate money for new draperies for the auditorium or tureens for the cafeteria. Once she had the money in hand it was spent on classrooms and books.

Durham was the national headquarters for black insurance companies, so it had a black middle class with higher incomes than in other southern cities. But having money in one's pocket did not win an exemption from Jim Crow, as two friends of Carol's were eager to show us. A young couple, both with good jobs, they took us to see their home in a segregated neighborhood, where the streets were unpaved and there were no sewers or garbage collection. They then insisted on driving us to the Chapel Hill airport, the only place in the state where the four of us could drink coffee together. Although so many years have passed, I still remember their eagerness to show us how they lived, as well as their cordiality. It was as if the humili-ations they encountered every day melted away instantly in the face of our sympathy. Surely that is the way that the black people we met in those years — in New York as well as in the South — must have been feeling. They were so accustomed to rudeness and rebuffs that our proffers of friendship and sympathy were accepted without question.

The trip to Durham and the encounter with Carol Bowie, who became a close friend, spurred me on to complete *Mary Jane*. I mailed in the manuscript, then waited anxiously for a reaction. Finally Peggy Lesser phoned to say that the book had been accepted and that Ernest Crichlow would do a cover and fron-tispiece. Later I learned through the company grapevine that the pros and cons of bringing out *Mary Jane* had been thoroughly discussed at an editorial meeting until editor-in-chief Kenneth McCormick had said, "It's time we bite the bullet."

I did not realize how courageous Doubleday was until years later, when the *Saturday Review of Literature* published *The All-White World of Children's Books* by Nancy Larrick, and I learned that at the same time that *Mary Jane* was being readied for publication, a writer whose book was already in galleys was forced to change the skin color of her leading character in answer to salesmen's objections. Pressure from jobbers had postponed still another book about minority children, and a book club had rejected a manuscript "because Southern subscribers would not like the way the heroine tackled the problem of prejudice." Even the illustrations in books about sports showed only white players.

Mary Jane was published in January 1959. The heavens did not fall and Doubleday was not boycotted, although at the annual Christmas party a salesman told me that it was as much as his life was worth to enter a Chicago bookstore with a book showing a black face on its jacket. *Mary Jane* won some minor awards but did not receive significant attention until after the sit-ins and freedom rides. The first notice came from abroad, where the book was published in England, Holland, Germany, Sweden, and Czechoslovakia; in 1964 the Soviet Union brought out an edition of 100,000 copies. Unlike the other countries whose publishers paid me royalties, the Soviet Union did not subscribe to the Universal Copyright Convention. A letter from Moscow informed me that I would receive 527 rubles, 40 kopeks (roughly $585) "if you come to the Soviet Union." I never went.

Sales mounted slowly in the United States, increasing after Scholastic Book Services, the largest publisher of children's books, brought it out in paperback. By the time the hardcover edition went out of print in the late 1970s, Scholastic had sold half a million copies and Doubleday, 76,000. A prominent children's book editor tells me that *Mary Jane* broke taboos. "I remember being overwhelmed that someone had finally written a book that was not idealized or prettified but that attempted to tell the truth," she said.

Did the book influence southern readers? Probably not. I had hoped to reach white children in places like Clinton to give them an insight into their black classmates' problems. However, at the height of *Mary Jane*'s popularity, when I was receiving ten letters a week from young readers, almost all came from the North. The book did become a favorite among black children, who for almost the first time found a dark-skinned heroine. In *Death at an Early Age*, Jonathan Kozol's first book, he wrote that when he was teaching in Boston he purchased two dozen copies of *Mary Jane* for his students, only to be told by his supervisor that "it wasn't fair to the white children in the class to force such books on them." Shortly afterward, when he compounded his sins by reading a Langston Hughes poem to his class, he was fired.

CHAPTER

12

By the late 50s life had become more relaxed. Peter was getting ready to go to Cornell and Anne was playing folk songs on her guitar and begging to be taken to hootenannies in New York. As the blacklist slowly lost its power, Phil not only felt more secure at CBS but even received a raise. We were able to pay off most of our house debt and begin to think of a vacation. Along with hundreds of others, we had been unable to obtain passports to travel abroad, because the State Department demanded to know if we were or had ever been communists. At last in 1958, the Supreme Court ruled, in the case of artist Rockwell Kent, that the government had no right to inquire into a citizen's beliefs. With some trepidation, we visited the Passport Office in Rockefeller Center. No one asked the are-you-or-have-you-ever-been question and the passports came through in short order.

In the summer of 1960, we traveled to Italy, where Phil's younger brother lived, to France, and then to Czechoslovakia to see friends from New York, Hilda and Herbert Lass, who had been living in Prague since

1948. This was our first visit to a socialist country, and we desperately wanted to admire it. We saw all the tourist spots and also traveled to new towns in Slovakia where the miners, the nation's aristocrats, lived in apartments equipped with refrigerators, TVs, and other modern appliances. Most impressive were the nursery schools, open ten hours a day, with child-sized furniture and toys far better than any in the United States. The plump, red-cheeked children looked as if they had escaped from *USSR in Construction* or a 1930s Soviet film.

Hilda and I had corresponded during their years abroad, writing in doublespeak, conscious of prying eyes on both sides of the Iron Curtain. Now they told us of the Slansky trial, the Czech version of the Soviet show trials, and the anti-Semitism of the 50s, which was a feature of the trials. We spent a morning with a children's book editor who had brought out *Freedom Train* and was preparing a Czech edition of *Mary Jane*. Prague bookstores contained many American as well as Russian titles, and we even found the *New York Times* in a hotel in Wenceslas Square.

Would we want to live in Czechoslovakia? No, but then we wouldn't want to live in Italy or France, either. The trip helped us to sort out what we thought impor-tant. Nursery schools and health care, yes. But they were not worth much without a First Amendment and a Bill of Rights.

Close to My Heart

Throughout this period I wrote a number of nature books with Winifred Lubell, an artist I had first met at summer camp in Maine. Winnie lived across the county in Croton with her husband and two sons, contemporaries of Peter and Anne. To research *The Story of Caves*, our first collaboration, we packed the four teenagers into her station wagon during an Easter vacation and toured the caves of Pennsylvania. Our next venture was *Creatures of the Night*, a report on the moths, beetles, crickets, and other insects who spread their wings, feed, and mate after sunset. *Caterpillars* was my favorite of the books Winnie and I did at this time. I was the only gardener in Westchester who planted parsley to attract parsley caterpillars and who encouraged fat tomato hornworms to chew on my tomato plants. Imitating an experiment I had read about in J. Henri Fabre's *Life of the Caterpillar*, I put a newly hatched Cecropia moth (one of the giant silkworm moths) in a cage on our terrace. That night we watched two large Cecropias visit her; days later she laid eggs, which hatched into tiny, hungry caterpillars. How had I known her sex? Easy. *She* laid the eggs after *he* inseminated her. Another answer might be — beginner's luck.

Before the Russians launched *Sputnik*, science in children's books had been skimpy. Now it was acceptable to explain the Linnaean system of classification and to use words like "metamorphosis" and "phototropic." To do this I had to educate myself, and I tackled textbooks on chemistry, physics, and biology in an effort to fill in the gaps in my education. Although *The Story of Caves* was reprinted by Scholastic, the other books did not sell as well as Mike's and my earlier photographic ones had done. Nevertheless, by 1960 or so I was receiving more than $10,000 in royalties annually and feeling rather pleased.

Meanwhile, the civil rights movement was moving into high gear and I searched for ways to contribute. I settled on a biography of Lucretia Mott, a Quaker who had fought against slavery and spoken out for women's rights. Her letters, in collections at Swarthmore and Smith Colleges, were my first introduction to the abolitionists who had reached out a hand to their black sisters and brothers. I also encountered Susan B. Anthony and Elizabeth Cady Stanton, pioneer women leaders. Stanton's great-granddaughter, Rhoda Jenkins, lived in Rye, and she took me to meet her mother, Nora Barney, who reminisced about her grandmother and even loaned me some of her books.

Before I finished *Lucretia Mott* I became personally involved in the civil rights struggle. When Bob Brown resigned from the presidency of the local NAACP, his place was taken by Orial Redd, a woman in her mid-thirties whose family had lived in Rye for four generations. She and her husband, Paul, and their small daughter lived in a three-room apartment off Midland Avenue, the only Rye neighborhood where blacks were accepted. She was pregnant and desperately needed a larger apartment. Would I help her? We tackled the problem experimentally, since in 1960 there were no guidelines to follow. Orial went to a real estate agent and was told that he had no rentals. I followed and was shown an apartment. Then I went to another office and learned of a rental—which evaporated when Orial appeared. We even tried going together and appealing to the conscience of the realtor. We had the dubious pleasure of learning from the realtor that although he had no prejudice, of course, his tenants would object if a Negro moved in. We then dropped the agents and went directly to the half-dozen or so garden apartments in Rye, starting with Rye Colony, which was located near the New Haven Railroad, hardly an exclusive neighborhood. This time our movements were carefully orchestrated. Orial, who had a beautifully modulated voice, phoned the Rye Colony superintendent and made a date to see a vacant apartment. She and Paul kept the appointment and were promptly turned away, the superintendent advising them that Negroes were happier living by themselves. As soon as they telephoned to me, I went to Rye Colony, saw the apartment and, drawing a deep breath, told the superintendent I would take it. After filling out an application, I gave him my check for the first month's rent.

I had no hesitation about taking the apartment, because we had consulted with the State Commission

Against Discrimination (SCAD) in New York and an official there had told us that under the new Metcalf-Baker law against discrimination in housing we had an airtight case. Orial, Paul, and I immediately drove to the SCAD office in White Plains to file a complaint. It was then that we learned that the law would not go into effect until September, five months in the future.

What should we do next? After weeks of telephone calls, we set up a meeting between the owner of Rye Colony and a group of Rye citizens, including several of his tenants. During a protracted discussion, he told us that although he personally had Negro friends, he would not rent an apartment to the Redds. When we reminded him that SCAD would soon forbid discrimination, he cheerfully replied, "The law has no teeth." He turned out to be right.

For five months and then five months more, we checked apartment houses in Rye. After my face became familiar to rental agents, Alice and other friends took over the checking. One morning she learned of a vacancy at Rye Wood Gardens, then raced around the corner, where the Redds were waiting. They drove to the apartment house in two minutes flat—only to be told that the apartment had been rented. They had acquired two lawyers, Paul Zuber, who had initiated the New Rochelle school desegregation case, and Bill Kunstler, taking on his first civil rights assignment. With their help the Redds filed a complaint with SCAD, but were informed that Rye Wood's owner could not be served with papers because he was ill and living in Florida. By then we were old hands, and I find among my notes: "russet hat with feather, tan overcoat, leather shoes, Opel car." I had spotted the "ill" owner outside his development. Months of motions and countermotions in court in White Plains followed. Finally SCAD decided in the Redds' favor and ordered Rye Wood Gardens to rent the next vacant apartment to them. Victory? Not at all. The owner, he of the russet hat, had sold the development in the intervening months; the order did not apply to the new purchaser.

Paul Jr. was born, and slept in a crib in the Redds' kitchen alongside his sister while his parents appealed to Rye's mayor and city council. The newly organized Northern Student Movement set up a picket line on their behalf. After still one more hearing before SCAD, Rye Colony's owner capitulated, and the Redds were permitted to rent a four-and-a-half room apartment in the development. Phil and I joined them there for a celebratory dinner in October 1962.

Meanwhile, sit-ins at segregated lunch counters and freedom rides to protest segregation in transportation in the South were making headlines. I had just seen newspaper photographs of bloody, disheveled freedom riders, beaten up by local vigilantes, when Peter telephoned from Cornell. He was going to join a freedom ride sponsored by the Congress of Racial Equality (CORE), which would travel by train to Jackson, Mississippi.

The next days were tense ones. On television we caught a glimpse of Peter in New Orleans, where he was attending a training session on non-violence. The young people were taught to keep their hands at their sides and fists unclenched no matter how great the provocation, a lesson that scarcely allayed our anxiety. The following morning, eight of them, five white and three black, got off the train in Jackson, Mississippi, entered the "white" waiting room together, and were arrested.

Relieved to hear that Peter was in jail and thus safe from mob attack, we were further reassured when Bill Kunstler, in Mississippi for CORE, telephoned to say that Peter was fine. The next day the *New York Times* carried a front-page story about the Mississippi freedom riders, and our phone rang steadily. The first caller was my father, to say reproachfully, "No one in our family was ever in jail." His mood changed when people congratulated him on his grandson's courage and sent money to pay Peter's fine. After Peter returned home, the NAACP Youth Council gave him an award, and the Port Chester *Item* published a picture of him with the Youth Council president. The photograph of the two young men, one black, one white, smiling at each other, seemed to hold out a promise for a better future.

Apparently not everyone felt the same way; a night or two later, Phil and I were awakened by the sound of gunshot. When we looked out of the window we saw a seven-foot cross burning in our front yard. Phil put out the fire with a garden hose before the police arrived, but the news quickly circulated. Rye's mayor declared the incident "disgraceful"; Rye's ministers preached sermons against it; and Rye's police chief promised to investigate "until the culprits are brought to answer for their dastardly crime."

Telegrams and letters poured in. Most were supportive, but there were some unpleasant ones. One enclosed a clipping from the *Item* showing Phil and me looking at the charred cross. "The name is not Jewish but the face is," said a scrawled note. Another, from the Minute Men, was a drawing of the cross hairs of a telescopic rifle sight with "TRAITORS BEWARE!" printed below it. Most annoying was a nightly phone call from a woman who launched into a tipsy harangue just after we had gone to bed. We did not guess her identity until more than a decade later, when Watergate investigators revealed that Martha Mitchell, wife of Attorney General John Mitchell, was a heavy drinker given to late night telephoning. In 1961, Martha and John Mitchell lived in Rye, less than a mile from our home.

On the surface, I bore up well under the publicity. I answered every letter and utilized every interview to

235

call attention to the discrimination against the Redds, who had not yet found an apartment, and to the plight of black people in the Jim Crow South. Underneath, however, I was hurting. Fifteen years earlier I had naively believed that Rye would become our home town, that our children and grandchildren would live there happily ever after. Even though I had espoused unpopular causes, I still expected my fellow townspeople to recognize that I was basically a good person, exercising my constitutional right to dissent. The burning cross, symbolizing hatred, marked the end of my innocence, and it seemed vitally important to know who my enemies were. But as the days stretched to weeks it became apparent that this "dastardly crime" was never to be solved. Or rather, whispers led us to believe that the police chief and others knew who the perpetrators were, but because they were young people from "good" families no one wanted to jeopardize their futures for the likes of us.

That's the way matters stood when we went to Cape Cod for a vacation. Driving across the bridge that separates the Cape from the mainland, the tensions of the past months suddenly wafted away and I sat back, relaxed, taking deep breaths of salt-laden air. A year earlier we had bought an acre of land overlooking Wellfleet Bay. During our vacation we began to plan a house there.

CHAPTER

13

The years when we were building in Wellfleet were a time of intense activity in the civil rights movement. Swimming pools were integrated in Florida, parks in Louisiana; black students entered the University of Alabama, and black children were attacked by police dogs in Birmingham. Medgar Evers was assassinated in Mississippi, and Martin Luther King, Jr. delivered his "I Have a Dream" speech in Washington. As the movement's goals shifted, northern college students, including my niece Ellen Lake, spent the summer of 1964 in Mississippi organizing freedom schools and helping blacks register to vote.

Although I longed to be in the thick of the struggle, I knew that I could accomplish more at the typewriter. During the freedom summer, I made weekly trips to the office of the Student Nonviolent Coordinating Committee (SNCC) in New York to deliver books I had collected for the schools and to learn how the work was progressing. But most of the time I worked to finish *Lucretia Mott: Gentle Warrior* and *Forever Free: The Story of the Emancipation Proclamation*. Published at the time of the Proclamation's centennial in 1963, the latter book, which was also illustrated by Ernest Crichlow, offered ten to twelve-year-olds a look at American history from the point of view of black people.

Phil and I joined with a group of children's book writers and editors, including Franklin Folsom, Mary Elting, Lilian Moore, and Milton Meltzer, to organize a Council on Interracial Books. The Council issued a quarterly bulletin to introduce "integrated" books and to criticize racist ones like *Little Black Sambo* and *Dr. Dolittle*. Its most significant activity was an annual contest for the best books and illustrations by minority artists. A number of talented young people were thus introduced to publishers; many remained to prosper in the field. In a short time, the Council became so successful that it was able to support a paid organizer, thereby giving Phil and me an excuse for skipping the meetings in New York.

Doubleday was the first major publisher to see the way the wind was blowing. At a formal luncheon in January 1964 the company launched Zenith Books, supplementary social studies texts with special emphasis on minorities. The concept was so new—black history for classrooms—that it got extra careful attention. Each book was to be prepared by a writer (white) and a historian (black); illustrations were by black artists, and a white reading specialist produced teachers' manuals. Overall consultant for the series was Dr. John Hope Franklin, later the chairman of the President's Council on Race but at that time chairman of the History Department at the University of Chicago. I had met Dr. Franklin, a friendly, witty man, at several Du Bois birthday dinners, including some when other black academicians deemed it prudent to stay away.

I was assigned to work with Dr. Benjamin Quarles of Morgan State College, the author of *The Negro in the American Revolution*, *The Negro in the Civil War*, a biography of Frederick Douglass, and other books. He wrote in such a pleasant popular style that I wondered why I was needed as co-author. My surmise is that the publisher felt so unsure of the project that it was deemed necessary to include white writers whose names would, presumably, have greater recognition for book buyers. Actually, the whites chosen were not a distinguished lot, while the black historians were all topflight people in their fields. Ben and I agreed on short biographies of Mary Church Terrell, Booker T. Washington, James Weldon Johnson, and W. E. B. Du Bois, to be titled *Lift Every Voice*. We rarely met, since he lived in Baltimore, but he sent me copies of hard-to-find articles and letters, while I went through books at the Schomburg Collection. Tactful as well as learned, Ben made no attempt to alter my interpretations, particularly of Du Bois, who had died in 1963. I included an account of his persecution during the McCarthy era and his decision, at the age of ninety-three, to join the Communist Party, telling these years as I had witnessed them, and neither Dr. Quarles nor Dr. Franklin asked for changes. *Lift Every Voice* was not only the first account of Dr. Du Bois's career for young readers, it was also the first book for classroom use that discussed the stifling of dissent in the 1950s.

Although my collaboration with Ben Quarles was a happy one, this was not true of all of the Zenith teams. One writer was so woefully ignorant of history that Dr. Rayford Logan, leading historian at Howard University, refused to work with her, and Phil was asked to take over the assignment. Their *Four Took Freedom* told the stories of Harriet Tubman, Robert Smalls, Frederick Douglass, and Blanche K. Bruce, the first black U.S. senator. With illustrations by Charles White, a noted black artist, it became Zenith's best-seller.

Phil had remained at CBS long enough to collect the traditional twenty-year gold watch, then had taken early retirement, setting himself up with a typewriter and telephone in Peter's old room. *Laughing on the Outside*, the anthology of Negro humor that he had been working on since the 1950s, had been turned down by publisher after publisher because "there's no market for books about blacks." Finally accepted by Grosset and Dunlap, its editors perceived it as a joke book rather than a serious historical survey and subtitled it *The Intelligent White Reader's Guide to Negro Tales and Humor.** The subtitle was exactly wrong in 1965, when book buyers wanted to hear from blacks, not whites. Reviews were scarce, and most of the edition made its way to the remainder tables in short order. A few copies reached university libraries so that it is occasionally cited in a footnote.

Phil was still licking his wounds when he wrote a second Zenith book, *The Quiet Rebels*, biographies of four Puerto Rican leaders, a project that gave us an excuse for a winter vacation in Puerto Rico. Anxious to get away from "baby books," he then asked me to work with him on a biography of Judge J. Waites Waring. Waring was a Charleston, South Carolina, aristocrat who had supported segregation until his appointment to the federal bench when, he explained, "I acquired a passion for justice." Turning his back on his past, his decisions opened the white primaries to black voters and equalized teachers' pay. He became the first judge in the nation to declare that "segregation is *per se* inequality," a dissenting opinion that led directly to the Supreme Court's 1954 school decision. Ostracized by old friends and even shot at, he finally retired from the bench and with his wife moved to

---

*Borrowed from George Bernard Shaw's "The Intelligent Woman's Guide to Socialism and Capitalism."

New York, to the Hyde Park Hotel on Madison Avenue, where my parents lived. A maid on her morning rounds told my mother of the new arrival, identifying Waring as "the man who freed the slaves." Mother knew better, but made it her business to introduce herself to the judge in the elevator and of course to tell him of her clever daughter who had written books about black people. Always courteous, the judge suggested that we pay him a visit. We took him at his word and called one Sunday afternoon, thus beginning one of the most rewarding friendships of our lives.

Despite attention from the civil rights community, the judge, then in his eighties, was lonely and bored. His wife was crippled by arthritis and confined to their apartment, so that he seemed glad to accompany us to the theater occasionally and to have us listen to his reminiscences — Phil with his tape recorder and I with my steno notebook. A raconteur with a felicitous turn of phrase, he told of growing up in a slave-owning family who "lived on rice and recollections," of his success in Charleston's top-drawer white society, and finally of the remarkable change that had overtaken him in his sixties when he had been appointed a federal judge. To learn more of Waring's background, we spent a week in Charleston, our first visit to the city since my pursuit of Robert Smalls. The most obvious signs of segregation were gone. We could invite the Warings' black friends, civil rights activists Septima

Clark and Ruby Cornwell, to lunch at our hotel. But the people the judge had grown up with, played bridge with, and worked with in the Democratic party sounded frightened or angry when we telephoned. Even his nephew, Thomas S. Waring, editor of the Charleston *News and Courier*, was "out of town" to us.

Back in New York, Phil wrote an outline and sample chapter on Judge Waring, only to have an editor advise him to postpone the biography because in 1967 the reading public was interested in black heroes, not white ones. Too easily discouraged, Phil closed the file drawers stuffed with information and went on to other projects. His only published account of the judge's life was a two-column obituary in the *New York Times* when the judge died the following year at the age of eighty-seven.

As I look back, I am surprised to see how readily I slipped into the role of researcher on the Waring book, taking down the judge's bon mots and typing the research. Certainly I did this out of love and loyalty to Phil, who was not only a better writer than I but who had supported my writing apprenticeship by plugging away at CBS. But I would have been willing to do any menial work for the privilege of spending long hours with Judge Waring, who, even in his mid-eighties, had not lost his wit or sharp turn of phrase. As I watched his craggy face light up, I felt that he was the first person I had ever met to whom I would apply the word "great." In the 60s, those intensely moral times, his life gave a positive answer to the question we had debated for decades and that was part of our belief in socialism—can you change human nature?

We were vacationing in our new Cape Cod house in the summer of 1966 when Congressman Adam Clayton Powell, chairman of the House Committee on Education, invited me to testify at hearings on the treatment of minorities in text and library books. As part of Lyndon Johnson's War on Poverty, Congress had passed an Elementary and Secondary Education Act, aimed at improving the education of underprivileged children in Appalachia as well as in urban ghettos. The act provided $100 million for texts, library books, and other instructional materials; local school districts were to spend an additional $150 million. As the leading black spokesman in Congress, Powell wanted to make sure that these vast sums of money would be spent on books that included Negroes and other minorities.

Although always uncomfortable at the thought of appearing in public, I worked out a little statement about "the truth gap" in children's literature that kept white as well as black students from learning the facts about American life. By the time I reached Washington, where Doubleday had booked a room for me at the Mayflower Hotel, I had Walter Mitty-like fantasies of rousing Congress and the nation to action.

The reality was somewhat different. Congressman Powell appeared briefly to open the hearing, then left for what were doubtless more important duties. No reporters or television cameras were in evidence, and the sole account of my testimony was a paragraph in *Publishers Weekly*. Most of the other witnesses were textbook publishers and school administrators who came hat-in-hand hoping to gloss over their lily-white past while describing the multi-ethnic readers planned for the future. As the lone writer present, I tried not to sound smug.

The next years saw an undignified scramble as publishers rushed to claim their share of the federal money. A textbook represented a large capital investment. Expecting a complete revision was like asking General Motors to design a new car. All sorts of halfway compromises were tried out. Inserts that told about Frederick Douglass or Booker T. Washington were glued into otherwise lily-white history texts. One publisher instructed his illustrator to blacken the face of every tenth person in the pictures, a device that became known as "Color-me-black." Another publisher issued three editions of a primer. In the first all the children were white; in the second some were black; in the third the children were white but the teachers wore nuns' garb. One edition for the South, one for urban schools in the North, and one for parochial schools.

Trade books, issued in smaller editions, could respond more quickly to the demand. Books with black people on their covers suddenly were welcome in bookstores, and, to my discomfort, I was in demand as a public speaker. An English professor at the University of Wisconsin who had read my testimony in the record of the Powell hearings brought me to Wisconsin to address a teachers' institute and, the following year, to speak at the annual convention of the National Council of Teachers of English. The latter was a challenge, because although I lacked an advanced degree or special expertise I was being asked to tell the country's leading English teachers what they had been doing wrong and how they could best correct their errors.

In preparation for this speech I spent a fortnight in the Teachers College library in New York analyzing the anthologies of literature used in high schools. I was not surprised to discover that book after book contained examples of British, French, Russian, and Chinese writings but not a single story or poem by an American black. The title of my talk was "What's Black and White and Read All Over?" After surveying thirty eight anthologies, my answer was, "Not much." I then mapped out a course that would include the work of such well-known writers as Langston Hughes, James Baldwin, Arna Bontemps, Gwendolyn Brooks, and younger novelists like John

A. Williams, Paule Marshall, John O. Killens, and Chester Himes.

I can't report that I received a standing ovation at the NCTE convention. Some members of the audience clearly resented having an outsider criticize them, but both speeches were published in the influential *English Journal,* and reprints were widely distributed. During the next years I found myself bringing a similar message to PTA groups and gatherings of teachers and librarians. These speaking assignments were unpaid except once — only once — when a publisher sent me an honorarium of $1,250 for a day-long conference at which an anthology of black poetry was planned. The hourly rate was impressive, but like so many projects from those days, the initial burst of excitement about books on blacks began to peter out, and the anthology was never published.

At Doubleday, Peggy Lesser had retired, and the new editor of Books for Young Readers, Georgess McHargue, proposed that I write about the civil rights movement. More than half of the book was a history of black people's lives and the long, long struggle for freedom waged in the law courts and on the streets. After describing "the children's crusade" in the fight for school integration, I reported on Martin Luther King's nonviolent movement and came down to the present with an account of the black power position that the young people of SNCC were articulating. *Tear Down the*

Walls! subtitled *A History of the Black Revolution in the United States,* was at the printer when Martin Luther King, Jr. was assassinated. There was barely time to insert a dedication to King and a brief afterword. Doubleday announced the publication of the book with a full-page ad in *Horn Book Magazine,* a review of children's literature, which featured my picture alongside the headline, "READ, BABY, READ!"

Once Upon a Time editing children's books was largely an ivory tower job. The editor spent most of his time in the land of little furry animals and enchanted princesses. Nowadays the Prince's hair is longer than Rapunzel's and they've both joined a picket line. And nowadays we have writers like Dorothy Sterling who know of and applaud the change.

Between 1954 and 1965 Mrs. Sterling wrote five books relating to the black fight for equality. Most of these books were greeted with the proverbial resounding silence. But in the years that followed the young readers themselves broke that silence. They *were* concerned, they were interested and Mrs. Sterling's books quietly began selling. At present, when the controversy over equality is greater than ever, Dorothy Sterling continues to write for young readers. Her latest book is TEAR DOWN

THE WALLS!, a history of the country's black protest movement which lets the facts speak for themselves without condescension or censorship.

The ad was flattering, but I recognized its roots in the bottom line. When I next called on Georgess, another editor beckoned me to his office to show me a guide to federal aid programs that he was editing. In a chapter on new school libraries the suggested basic book list included an extraordinary number of Doubleday titles, among them many of my own. The editor could hardly keep from laughing at his clever sales gimmick while I struggled to hide my discomfort. The War on Poverty, the first federal program since the 1930s that was aimed at helping poor people, was also going to fill my pockets.

Although my royalty checks tripled, my enthusiasm for the War on Poverty began to fade in the face of President Johnson's other war, the war in Vietnam. After the commitment of ground forces to that faraway Asian country, a fledgling peace movement began a struggle against the war. Students demonstrated, burned their draft cards, and fled to Canada. Though our immediate family was not affected — Peter had a student deferment and Anne's husband was not a citizen — we of course sympathized with the war resisters, as did all of our friends. Jeanne Webber was a founder of Women's Strike for Peace. My father and my brother-in-law, Leonard Lake, advised young men how to avoid the draft and were paid with wrinkled joints of marijuana. *I Have Seen War*, an anthology of anti-war writings that I had edited for Hill and Wang in 1960, was reprinted by Popular Library. Phil and I went to New York for protest parades down Fifth Avenue and to Washington for a March on the Pentagon, where we held wet washcloths over our faces as tear gas canisters were lobbed at us.

In late May 1970, we went to Providence to see Anne receive her Ph.D. in biology from Brown. Days earlier four students had been killed at Kent State University during a protest against the U.S. invasion of Cambodia. Their deaths touched off strikes and demonstrations at colleges across the country. Even on Brown's usually staid campus, banners hung from dormitory windows and students handed out leaflets to passersby. We took our seats on the college green in the section roped off for parents. After the graduating seniors received their degrees, the doctoral candidates walked one by one to the platform. When the provost slipped Anne's hood over her head she turned so that everyone could read the sign fastened to the front of her gown: END THE WAR IN VIETNAM. The parents seated around us gasped. We felt proud.

Whenever the pushes and pulls of those turbulent years became overwhelming, we retreated to Wellfleet.

I swam in the bay and the ponds, jumped the waves in the ocean, walked the tidal flats, and started a small garden. Revived by the breeze from the salt marsh, I began thinking about a book on Cape Cod. Doubleday had recently teamed up with the Museum of Natural History to publish under the imprint of the Natural History Press. The editors agreed to a "family book" that would include not only the Cape, Martha's Vineyard, and Nantucket but also Block Island and the southeastern tip of Long Island, all lands that had been formed when the Ice Age glaciers retreated. Winnie Lubell, as enthusiastic as I about the Cape, worked with me during summer vacations, with occasional spring and fall forays. The Cape Cod National Seashore had been established in 1961; the park rangers took us by boat and jeep to places we might not have discovered on our own.

By the time *The Outer Lands: A Natural History Guide to Cape Cod, Martha's Vineyard, Nantucket, Block Island, and Long Island* was published in 1967, Phil, too, was deep in ecology, working on a biography of Rachel Carson, whose *Silent Spring* had alerted the world to the dangers of the chemicals that were poisoning the environment. The book was for a new "Women in America" series that Milton Meltzer was editing for T. Y. Crowell. Carson had died in 1964, so Phil's first telephone call was to Marie Rodell, Carson's literary agent and close friend. To his dismay, Rodell told him that he positively must not write the book. She planned to invite a prestigious author to write a definitive biography. The first book about Carson must not come from a virtually unknown writer doing a biography for young people. Encouraged by Milton and their editor at Crowell, Phil went ahead anyway. Rodell did her best to make his job difficult by asking Carson's friends not to meet him, but almost everyone ignored her advice. Robert Carson, Rachel's brother, her childhood friends, and the people she worked with at the Fish and Wildlife Service were all glad to talk with him and lend him photographs and old letters (which Rodell would not allow him to quote from).

I did not accompany Phil on his interviews in Pennsylvania and Washington, but when he went to Duxbury, across Cape Cod Bay from Wellfleet, I rode along. Olga Huckins, an old friend of Carson's, had a backyard bird sanctuary there—until the day in 1957 when a mosquito control plane flew over the town spraying DDT indiscriminately. Some fourteen of Huckins' bird visitors were dead, and they "died horribly, bills gaping open, claws drawn up to their breasts in agony," Huckins wrote Carson. Didn't Rachel know people in Washington who could stop future spraying? she asked. In 1957, DDT was still thought of as a miracle chemical, backed by a billion-dollar industry, but Rachel was immediately caught up by the challenge. She spent the next five years working with scientists across the country to ascertain and then prove the dangers to all forms of life posed by DDT. Olga Huckins had died by the time we visited Duxbury, but her backyard was there, still cluttered with bird baths and feeders. Recalling her letter, we felt almost mystically in touch with the birth of *Silent Spring*, the book that had changed the world.

Later that summer I accompanied Phil to Maine to see Carson's summer home and to meet Dorothy Freeman, her closest friend and neighbor. Dorothy — we were on first name terms immediately — showed us Rachel's woods, the beach where she had collected tiny sea creatures to study under a microscope when she was writing *The Edge of the Sea*, and the bay in which her ashes had been scattered after her death. Dorothy gave us a copy of Rachel's last letter to her. Rachel knew she was dying when she recalled a migration of Monarch butterflies that they had watched together and compared the insects' brief life cycles with her own, reminding Dorothy that when a life has run its course it was natural and not unhappy to have it come to its end. The moving letter made a perfect coda for Phil's book, but Marie Rodell flatly refused permission to publish it. He did his best with a paraphrase. When his *Sea and Earth: The Life of Rachel Carson* was published in 1970, it quickly became the most popular book in the Women of America series. The following year it won a Christopher Award for "artistic excellence in affirming the highest values of the human spirit."

Despite the pleasure I found in our ecology studies, I was still absorbed in the black revolution. I no longer felt welcome in SNCC's New York office, where Stokeley Carmichael and his associates were calling for black power. However, to show my sympathy for their position, I chose as subject for a biography Martin Delany, a 19th-century black nationalist who had been a physician, a major in the U.S. Army, and an African explorer. His friend Frederick Douglass said of him, "I thank God for making me a man, but Delany thanks Him for making him a *black man*." In his youth Delany had read medicine under white physicians and had made a precarious living as a cupper and bleeder. Hoping to complete his medical education, he applied to medical schools but was rejected. At last, in 1850, Dr. Oliver Wendell Holmes, dean of the Harvard Medical School, reluctantly admitted Delany and two other black men to Harvard. Fellow students immediately protested their presence, and they were expelled after three months.

The Harvard Medical School story had never been told. When I wrote to the school's Countway Library, asking permission to read the faculty minutes about the incident, my letter was unanswered. During a follow-up phone call, the curator of rare books and manuscripts explained with embarrassment that

Harvard officials did not want me to see the records. Because the medical school was situated at the edge of Boston's black ghetto, officials feared that the disclosure of this century-old racist incident might touch off a riot. But the curator was a scholar who did not believe in suppressing information, and I was persistent. During a day at Countway, I did not *see* the records, but he patiently read them aloud, pausing to give me time to take detailed notes. No riots followed publication of the book. Many decades later, when Harvard Medical School mounted a retrospective exhibition, a portrait of Martin L. Delany was prominently displayed as an early student. Its caption failed to explain that his Harvard education had lasted only three months.

A pleasant aspect of the work on the Delany book was my association with Victor and Louise Ullman. A former newspaperman, Victor was writing a biography of Delany for Beacon Press with the assistance of Louise, a librarian. Because their book was for adults and mine for young readers we felt no conflict and pooled our research. I gave him copies of the Harvard notes; he sent me photocopies of the first issues of Delany's newspaper, *The Mystery*, and filled me in on Delany's years in Canada. When the granddaughter of an early biographer of Delany loaned me her grandmother's journal, Louise deciphered the hard-to-read manuscript and made neatly typed copies. Toward the end of our research we were joined by Floyd J. Miller, a doctoral candidate who had discovered long-lost chapters of Delany's novel, *Blake*. He shared them with us and we opened our files to him. In the cutthroat academic and literary world, our relationship seemed unique, and we took pride in it. Long after the completion of our books, Phil and I visited the Ullmans on their mountaintop in New Hampshire, and they came to see us on Cape Cod.

My book was published in 1971 and reprinted by Da Capo Press in 1996. Throughout the period I was working on it, I was juggling other projects. Because publishers were suddenly enthusiastic about black books, I became an editorial consultant for Doubleday, Beacon, and Scholastic. At Doubleday I edited Perspective Books, a series of biographies of black notables for high school readers. Black novelists John A. Williams and John O. Killens covered the lives of Richard Wright and Denmark Vesey, leader of a slave revolt in 1822; Addison Gale, a young critic, wrote a biography of poet Paul Laurence Dunbar.*

At the same time I convinced our old friend Gobin Stair, editorial director of Beacon Press, that there were black history source books that cried out for pub-

---

* *The Most Native of Sons: A Biography of Richard Wright*, by John A. Williams; *Great Gittin' Up Morning: A Biography of Denmark Vesey*, by John Killens; *Oak and Ivy: A Biography of Paul Laurence Dunbar*, by Addison Gayle, Jr.

lication. Working with editor Arnold Tovell, we reprinted Arna Bontemps' *Black Thunder*, an account of Gabriel Prosser's 1800 slave revolt, and Bontempss collection *Great Slave Narratives*. I importuned Dorothy Porter to put together a book from her bulging files of early pamphlets, broadsides, and articles. Working with Dorothy was a joy, but she was a perfectionist who found it hard to stop without including every fact and rechecking every name and date. Finally we met in Boston for a night of last-minute editing in the Parker House; she reluctantly gave the manuscript to Arnold Tovell over breakfast the next morning. *Early Negro Writing 1760–1837*, published in 1971, still remains a basic collection of documents that illuminates the early experience of black people on this continent. Black Classics Press reprinted the book in 1995.

Other Beacon books on which I worked included *The Trial Record of Denmark Vesey*, with an introduction by John Killens, and *The New York Conspiracy*, a 1744 account of the prosecution of more than 170 slaves and white persons accused of conspiring against the colonial government. The book was edited by Thomas J. Davis, a young black historian who, fourteen years later, gave his own report of the conspiracy in *A Rumor of Revolt: "The Great Negro Plot" in Colonial New York*.

The emphasis on slave revolts in both series of books was not accidental. The rhetoric of revolution was in the air in those days. The well-behaved young people who had espoused nonviolence were now lined up behind SNCC's Rap Brown, who declared that "Violence is as American as cherry pie," or were supporting the Black Panthers, whose slogan of "Power to the People" was backed with guns and talk of revolution. White students opposed to the war in Vietnam were equally revolutionary in their sentiments. Consequently, when novelist William Styron published *The Confessions of Nat Turner*, a fictional account of a slave rebel, I hastened to buy a copy.

Nat Turner had been a slave preacher who, like Joan of Arc, heard voices commanding him to free his people. In 1831 he marched through the Virginia countryside with a small band of disciples, killing planters and their families, until the militia put down the revolt. Turner was hanged, but to the slaves he remained a legend—Prophet Nat, who would return someday to set them free.

Writing in the first person, as if Turner were narrating the story, Styron invented his own version of the slave leader. Ignoring the few known facts—that Turner came from a close-knit family who had taught him to read, that he had a slave wife—Styron's Nat was an irresolute Hamlet-like character whose life had been shaped by a kindly master and who lusted after the milky-white flesh of a planter's daughter. His rebellion was sparked not by hatred of slavery but instead by repressed sexual desires. Nowhere had Styron portrayed the messianic leader who was still revered by blacks.

Although the book was a selection of the Book-of-the-Month Club, topped best-seller lists, and won a Pulitzer Prize, Phil and I read it with mounting distaste. We saw it as a blundering attempt by a white Virginian to belittle a black rebel and reply to the black power movement. Its acceptance by critics and readers implied that there was still a significant lack of understanding between black and white intellectual spokesmen.

I was steaming about Styron's novel when John A. Williams phoned and judged the book even more harshly than I had. After a similar conversation with John Henrik Clarke, who had recently lectured on black history to the Rye Council for Human Rights, I telephoned Arnold Tovell in Boston to suggest that Beacon offer blacks a forum to reply to Styron. Arnold flew to New York the next day to have dinner with Clarke and me at the Harvard Club, his residence when he was in the city. I was always amused by the conferences with Arnold at the Harvard Club, where men entered by the front door while I was required to use the side-door Ladies' Entrance and to be formally escorted to meet my host. After I meekly made my way to the dining room, the three of us got down to business. As editor of *Freedomways* magazine, Clarke had a broad acquaintance among black intellectuals. He proposed inviting ten writers to comment on Styron's book, with the stipulation that no one at Beacon edit or amend their essays. Although this was an unusual concession for a publisher to make, it was so much in the mood of the times—that blacks must speak for themselves—that Beacon accepted it. Royalties were to be divided between Clarke and his contributors. Having completed my mission, I withdrew from the project.

William Styron's Nat Turner: Ten Black Writers Respond was published in the summer of 1968. The 120-page book included essays by John A. Williams and John Killens, English professor Mike Thelwell, psychiatrist Alvin Poussaint, and Lerone Bennett, editor of *Ebony*. Although the essays were sometimes repetitious and occasionally polemical, they reflected what Clarke wrote in his preface: "No event in recent years has touched and stirred the black intellectual community more than Styron's novel."

Instead of sympathizing with the pain that the black writers felt because Styron had distorted their hero, the white literary establishment lined up solidly against them. On the front page of the *Times* Book Review, in a two-part review in the daily *Times*, and in a lengthy critique in the *New York Review of Books*, the black writers were lambasted and Styron's right to use history imaginatively in order to create a "larger truth" stoutly defended.

That fall, I went to the forty-third annual meeting of the Association for the Study of Negro Life and

History. In the past the meetings of this venerable organization were small affairs attended by black scholars and a handful of white history buffs like me. In 1968 the lounge and meeting rooms of the New York Hilton Hotel were filled with white faces. Editors and literary agents were pursuing black writers, waving contracts. The atmosphere was cordial, if slightly frantic, until lunch was served. Then Arthur Schlesinger, Jr., professor of history following a stint as a White House advisor, warned the audience against "bad history inspired by group resentment and pride [that] often succumbed to the temptation of overstatement." He mentioned no names, but everyone understood that the "bad history" referred to *Ten Black Writers Respond*. The speech was met with muted applause, and I thought I detected somewhat less cordiality between blacks and whites after lunch than there had been before. The controversy quickly spread to Hollywood, where a producer who had paid $600,000 for the film rights to Styron's book shelved the project after listening to criticism from black spokesmen.

Speaking at a PEN awards ceremony on the thirtieth anniversary of the publication of *The Confessions of Nat Turner*, William Styron was still resentful. *Ten Black Writers Respond*, he lamented, was being taught in black studies courses while his novel was ignored. There were some who thought he just didn't get it.

My third venture as an editor began when Scholastic Book Services asked Milton Meltzer and me to serve as editors of Firebird Books, a multi-ethnic history and biography series. Milton, a friend and colleague since the 1950s, when he wrote *A Pictorial History of the Negro People* in collaboration with Langston Hughes, edited the history books and I the biographies. Intended for use in third and fourth grade social studies classes, the books were to include Native Americans, Hispanics, and Asians as well as blacks. With teachers' guides prepared by a board of educational consultants, Firebird would be the most impressive challenge to date to the all-white world of children's books.

Given a free hand, Milton and I contracted for books on the black soldiers of the American Revolution, black leaders before and after the Civil War, the expulsion of the Cherokee from their homeland, Hispanics in the Southwest, and the seldom-told story of the detention of Japanese-Americans during World War II. It was an unusual selection of topics for elementary school readers, far broader than what any textbook covered. Finding writers proved difficult. Although we signed up authors of children's books, journalists, novelists, and even a poet, we discovered that not every literate person could produce the kind of easy-to-read, high-action book that Scholastic, with its broad audience, required. One writer quit, another was dropped, a third demanded that his name be removed from the book because Scholastic's editor had chopped his sentences in half and blue-penciled his fine flourishes. Milton and I wrote, rewrote, and tried to keep the peace, while Scholastic's art department did an outstanding job of collecting old prints and photographs for illustrations.

By 1972 we had a dozen books in print, complete with Teachers' Guides and promotional posters for schools. Not all were great literature, but they were nothing to be ashamed of either. Such well-known children's book writers as Anne Terry White and Ann McGovern had written *The False Treaty: The Removal of the Cherokees from Georgia* and *The Defenders: Osceola, Tecumseh, Cochise*. Milton had done a picture history of Reconstruction, *To Change the World;* Phil had produced *A Question of Color,* which included biographies of Marcus Garvey and Malcolm X; my book *It Started in Montgomery* was a picture history of the civil rights movement.

Long before the final books appeared in print, Milton and I were busy with other projects. Only after several royalty statements did we realize that the books were not selling well or, rather, that they were not selling at all. Scholastic never notified us that they had killed the series, but when Milton visited the office one day, an executive apologetically said, "The teachers did not like them." Equally compelling, no doubt, was that President Nixon and his Congress did not like the War on Poverty or federal money spent on multi-ethnic books.

Probably the Firebird Books were pulped, standard practice when publishers were faced with an over-stock. But I occasionally dream that in a dusty ware-house in the Bronx there are tens of thousands of these books on America's minorities that someone will dis-cover. Someday.

CHAPTER

14

Despite my involvement with black writers, my conscience was troubling me. Rap Brown, Eldredge Cleaver, Huey Newton, and other black radicals were saying what Frederick Douglass had told the abolitionists more than a century earlier: "We must be our own advocates." Should I continue to write about black history? During my reading of 19th-century black newspapers and books, I had encountered many people whose stories begged to be told. And I knew of dozens of untapped sources, ranging from the archives of local historical societies and black churches to the National Archives, whose vast holdings about black people had not yet been investigated. I wanted to write about Paul Cuffe, the 18th-century sea captain; James McCune Smith, the first university-trained black doctor; Maria Stewart, who lectured in Boston in 1835; sailmaker James Forten and his daughters, poet and novelist Frances Ellen Watkins Harper; Mary Ann Shadd Cary, "editress" of a black newspaper; and so on.

While working on the Doubleday and Scholastic series, I had tried to share my sense of discovery with young black writers, but they had their own interests to pursue. At last I compromised with my conscience by collecting and annotating two books of black writings that would sample the available sources. The first, *Speak Out in Thunder Tones: Letters and Other Writings by Black Northerners, 1787–1865*, published in 1973, contained letters, journals, and newspaper articles, including an 1802 song about Thomas Jefferson and Sally Hemings. I added a biographical directory listing more than fifty women and men whose lives I hoped future researchers would investigate.

Using a desk-sized microfilm reader that had recently come on the market, I purchased the Library of Congress's reels of early black newspapers and made microfilm or Xerox copies of documents in other archives, so that I was able to work at home. But where was home? As the 60s drew to a close I sometimes fantasized that the Pied Piper had marched along Kirby Lane North with his flute, summoning all inhabitants. Not only were the children who used to gather in our kitchen off to college and careers, but their parents had gone, too. Mike and Ann Ehrenberg were in New York, a short walk from Zabar's. The Wrights were in Kansas, and Jeanne Webber, now riddled with cancer, had an apartment in the West Village. Although I went to New York for dinner with Jeanne and still had my weekly lunch with Alice, I missed the old community where children and casserole dishes seemed to have common ownership and there was always someone to talk with about the state of the world. To add to my discontent, our house was too big, and the heating system was as noisy as ever. I was ready for a move, preferably to Cape Cod, but Phil was difficult to uproot. He enjoyed writing at home and working with the NAACP and other neighborhood organizations. Thoroughly urban, he declared in his emphatic way that he never wanted to be more than forty minutes from a corned beef sandwich at the Gaiety delicatessen on Broadway. We might have remained deadlocked indefinitely had it not been for Nelson Rockefeller.

In his fifth term as governor of New York, Rockefeller proposed a bridge across Long Island Sound with the access road directly in front of our property. We would face a cacophony of squealing brakes and shifting gears, while our once clear air turned blue from exhaust fumes. We immediately put our house on the market. Although property in the neighborhood had appreciated considerably in the twenty years that we had lived there, we thought ourselves lucky when we were able to sell the house for approximately what it had cost. Ironically, the bridge never was built; the Department of the Interior finally banned it on environmental grounds.

Peter, his wife, Ellen, and their baby daughter, Emily, had recently moved to Philadelphia. I here, Peter was teaching in the University of Pennsylvania's Medical School and Ellen was starting a practice in psychology and, not incidentally, having a second child, Daniel. Anne and her husband, Nelson Fausto, were in the department of biology and medicine at Brown University. Much as we loved our children, we never considered moving to Philadelphia or Providence. Since Phil still clung to his urban roots, we rented a townhouse in a development in Greenwich, Connecticut, across the state line from Port Chester and within commuting reach of the Gaiety corned beef sandwich. In Rye it had been difficult to get repairmen; here a phone call brought a carpenter or a plumber immediately. A gardener weeded the foundation plantings and swept the steps and paths. It was hard to imagine a more perfect set-up. We should have been deliriously happy—but we weren't.

Jake, our headstrong black poodle, who was accustomed to the freedom of Kirby Lane North, had to be walked on a leash. The view from our living room window was dominated by the Greenwich incinerator, which emitted great clouds of black smoke throughout the day. At night the poorly insulated party wall enabled us to hear the neighbors bickering, their babies crying, their barking dog. After two years, when the landlord raised the rent to $400 a month, a sum we considered outrageous, even Phil was ready for Cape Cod.

During the decade that we had owned a house in Wellfleet we had continued to think of the place as "Escape Cod." We were summer people associating with summer people, unconcerned about politics, local or national, when we were there. Only twice in those years was our carefree existence threatened. One September, as we were getting ready to leave the Cape, friends telephoned from New York. Rap Brown, then high on the FBI's wanted list, was badly in need of a vacation. Could he stay in our house after we left? Rap Brown, whose shock of black hair and oversized sunglasses were then familiar to every television viewer, would be highly visible in Wellfleet, where black people were a rarity. How would we explain his presence to the neighbors with whom we spent moonlit nights on the beach drinking (too much) and singing old songs? What would we say to our builder, who acted as caretaker in the winter? Or to the postmistress, whose friendly smile contrasted so with the postal clerks in Rye?

But the call had come from a couple from Time Inc. days. Among the few whites still working with black radicals, they had recently taken out a mortgage on their home to raise bail for the Black Panthers. Phil and I discussed the pros and cons of their request, but our answer was never in doubt. Unhappily we said "yes." For once a good deed went unpunished. Rap Brown's plans changed and he never came to Wellfleet.

The second threat to our serenity came late one winter, when we were still in the New York area. A Wellfleet neighbor telephoned to report hills of sand in the marsh north of our property with a bulldozer poised to spread them. When we had bought the land the developer had assured us that this marsh could never be filled in because it was protected by new federal and state wetlands laws. The marsh could not be filled, but that was just what was happening.

Throwing an overnight bag and Jake into the back of our station wagon, we drove hellbent for Wellfleet. The bulldozer operator had left for the day when we arrived, but there was still time to alert *The Cape Codder*, the local weekly. The following day a photographer from the paper documented the presence of the bulldozer and we called on the chairman of the Wellfleet Conservation Commission. A day later the bulldozer was gone before we got up in the morning. Three decades have passed and the hills of sand, now covered with bearberry vines and with an occasional pitch pine growing at a summit, are still discernible along the edge of the marsh.

The incident gave us an introduction to Cape Cod in winter, when the quaint fishing village that tourists admired operated under a system of frontier justice. If someone wanted to fill a marsh or cut down a tree that blocked his view he did it in January or February, when summer people were not around to bear witness. Anyone who observed the deed kept silent or, in true Yankee fashion, admired its "cuteness."

In Wellfleet no one was "cuter" than Charles Frazier, the town's only lawyer and largest real estate developer. In early decades he had been chairman of the board of selectmen. Now he was town moderator and town counsel. In the 1950s he had helped bring the town a multi-million-dollar marina, financed by the state and federal funds. No one ever mentioned that a jury had convicted him of a "sweetheart" deal in connection with the marina's construction, although he had gotten off without punishment on appeal.

Instead everyone talked about favors Charlie had done for them. In the beauty parlor on Main Street where I went for haircuts, women sitting under hair dryers unconsciously raised their voices. I was not intentionally eavesdropping when I heard one woman say that Charlie prepared her income tax "and I didn't have to pay a cent"—while another reported that Charlie had gotten her real estate tax reduced. Field Point, where we had built our house, had been developed by Frazier and his partner, Robert Lesser. Undoubtedly they were responsible for the bulldozer and its surreptitious removal.

Although we had lost a little of our innocence when we finally moved to Wellfleet in the spring of 1973, we were prepared to believe a former New Yorker who had preceded us when he said that we were joining a classless society where carpenters, plumbers, fisher-men sent their children to the same school and had an equal say at town meeting. New Englander town meeting—the last bastion of American democracy, wasn't it? Well, not exactly. As moderator—the equiv-alent of chairman—Charles Frazier gave the floor to his friends and ignored the other waving hands. He cut short a speech he preferred not to hear, and when a vote was taken it was he who decided for the "ayes" or "nays." He had Robert's Rules of Order at his finger-tips and was adept at utilizing them. He was outra-geous, autocratic, and so witty and charming that he carried most of his audience with him. We had read about Boston politicians like Honey Fitz and James Michael Curley. Charlie Frazier was Wellfleet's "Last Hurrah."

Over the next months, as we joined a food coopera-tive whose members purchased inexpensive vegetables and held potluck suppers in a drafty tavern on the waterfront, we met a group of young people, many of them from the student movement of the 60s, who had come to the Cape seeking the simple life. From them we learned that Karl Marx and our exurban friend had gotten it wrong. Wellfleet and the neighboring town of

Truro were made up of three classes: the Born Heres, the Wash-Ashores, and the Summer People. From Memorial Day to Labor Day the Summer People were petted and pampered; their taxes and purchases supported the town's economy. During the rest of the year they were ignored; they had no vote in town meeting or local elections. The Born Heres, some of whose families dated back to the 17th century, had always run the town. But in recent years an increasing number of newcomers were beginning to speak on local issues. Although these fugitives from the cities wore blue jeans and flannel shirts and drove pickup trucks, they were still Wash-Ashores, never fully accepted by the Born Heres. A story was told about a town meeting at which a speaker insisted that he was a Cape Codder. "I've lived here for forty years," he said. "My children were born here." A voice from the rear interrupted: "If a cat has kittens in the oven, that don't make them biscuits."

The debates between the two groups might have remained amicable had it not been for the concerns about the environment that the Wash-Ashores brought with them. Still preferring to run things as their fathers had done, the Born Heres grumbled about new zoning restrictions and laws protecting wetlands. Their gut feeling that a man had a right to do what he wanted with his own property had been exacerbated when the Cape Cod National Seashore was established, over

Charles Frazier's strenuous objections. Wash-Ashores believed that the seashore had saved the lower Cape from the razzle-dazzle urban sprawl that spoiled the shores of New Jersey and Long Island. Many Born Heres felt that the seashore's restrictions deprived them of a chance to sell their ancestral lands at a good profit.

Phil and I determined not to get entangled in local politics. He was finishing *The Real Teachers*, a collection of interviews with teachers who were successful in inner-city schools. The book was published by Random House, where Phil's editor was Toni Morrison, whose first novel, *The Bluest Eye*, was receiving favorable attention. I was working on my second source book, a collection of documents from the Reconstruction period. I had spent weeks at the National Archives going through the records of the Freedmen's Bureau as well as thousands of letters and interviews with blacks from the post–Civil War period. These, read in conjunction with two dozen volumes of Congressional investigations of conditions in the South, gave me material for several years' work. If there were gaps in the microfilm and Xerox records, the Boston Library was only twenty-five minutes away by plane from Provincetown. In those halcyon days of Cape air travel I could put in a 9-to-5 day at the library for a round-trip fare of $35. And on good days when I was the only passenger on the plane, the pilot would fly low so that I could see a pod of whales breaching in Cape Cod Bay. Eventually I fashioned the Xeroxes and microfilm into *The Trouble They Seen: Black People Tell the Story of Reconstruction*. Illustrated with contemporary drawings and photographs, *Trouble* was the longest and most scholarly of the books I had done. After its publication in 1976, the National Council for the Social Studies gave it their Carter G. Woodson Book Award. Da Capo Press reprinted it in 1994.

Despite our good intentions, we were like fire horses put to pasture who neighed and pawed the ground when the firebell rang. Phil could not keep silent at town meeting in 1975 when the selectmen were asked for funds to spray the trees along town roads in an attempt to wipe out gypsy moths. Drawing on his biography of Rachel Carson, he pointed out that indiscriminate spraying posed a threat to people and to the Cape's water supply while doing little to stop the moths. After angry rebuttals from many in the audience, including a representative of the firm that did the spraying, his motion was defeated. The following year, however, he had supporters—Wash-Ashores all. The meeting again approved the budget for spraying but voted to appoint a Pesticide Study Committee. In the days after town meeting loud guffaws could be heard in the corridor of Town Hall. The selectmen had appointed a pesticide committee and, one observer said, "had put all the pests on it." The laughter died down after Phil and the other members wrote such a well-documented report that it became a model for towns all over Massachusetts. In subsequent years, Wellfleet slashed its budget for pest control.

Pesticides were not the only environmental dispute. The town dumped boulders and rubble along a narrow stretch of coast in a misguided attempt at erosion control. Marshes were filled so that homes could be constructed despite laws protecting wetlands. These actions were undertaken with the permission of the Conservation Commission, whose members were appointed by the selectmen, all Charlie Frazier partisans.

A major controversy arose over the recently constructed dike at the mouth of the Herring River whose sluice gate could be regulated to permit more or less salt water to reach the river valley. Shellfishermen and conservationists favored more water; real estate interest led by Frazier wanted the dike closed to protect property upstream. Emotions ran so high that we felt as if we were characters in a real-life mystery story where at any moment the crank that operated the sluice gate might disappear. Or the dike would be blown up one moonless night. Or someone would shoot Ace Jones.

C. Jones, a Field Point neighbor, was a retired business executive who was pouring his considerable intelligence and energy into protecting Wellfleet's environment. President of the newly organized Association for the Preservation of Cape Cod, he sent scathing letters to the local papers, handed out equally sharp leaflets at meetings, and petitioned the state to enforce its environmental laws. But even after the state's Department of Quality Engineering (DEQE) ordered the town to open the sluice gate wider, Town Counsel Frazier advised the selectmen to ignore the order.

Our friendship with Ace was unusual; he was a republican who had voted for Nixon for President. We never discussed national politics, as Phil tried tactfully to tone down his inflammatory letters and I wrote "Our Cape Cod Salt Marshes," a pamphlet distributed by the APCC. Ace was so unpopular at Town Hall that Charlie Frazier had him arrested for an alleged violation of the election laws. After a policeman appeared at his door with a warrant for his arrest, we helped organize a "Free Ace Jones" committee and accompanied him to court. The judge dismissed the case, commenting wryly that as a district judge he had never before been privileged to rule on a free speech issue. We paid our dues too when the Conservation Commission forbade us to repair our road, claiming, tongue-in-cheek, that repairs would damage the marsh—the same marsh that we had saved from Frazier's bulldozer. Only when we took photographs showing that the puddles in the road after a rain reached my boot tops were we permitted to fill the potholes.

While Ace issued his biting diatribes, the young people of the food co-op and other Wash-Ashores turned to electoral politics. The three-man board of selectmen appointed the town committees. If we could elect two selectmen not beholden to Frazier, we could turn the town around. We pored over election lists, built a card file of registered voters, called meetings to explain the issues. While Phil utilized his CBS training to write press releases and candidates' speeches, I served on the telephone squad that canvassed voters. After years of diligent work, first one, then two independent selectmen were elected. Finally in 1983 a majority of the members of the Conservation Committee believed in conservation. The crank that operated the Herring River dike was turned over to DEQE and Charles Frazier retired as town counsel.

The environmental wars were won by hard work, diligent politicking—and a change in demography. During the decade, the antiVietnam warriors of the 60s had been joined by new immigrants: college professors, scientists, artists, and writers who chose Wellfleet and Truro rather than Miami or Phoenix for retirement homes. Most were city folk who at first thought of marshes as swamps where mosquitoes bred, but they were quick learners. Wellfleet soon adopted a charter form of government with a paid administrator.

Close to My Heart

The expanded population and fattened tax rolls enabled the town to build a new police and fire station and, important for retired people, a splendid new library. The end of cronyism also brought restrictions on former liberties. The dump became a sanitary land-fill where recycling was required. Motor vehicles were forbidden on the beaches, motorboats on the ponds, and licenses were mandated for shellfishing and beach parking. Throughout the struggle Phil and I had been uncomfortably aware of some condescension expressed by the city-dwellers turned year-rounders. We felt sympathetic with the Born Heres who were losing their old privileges. When Phil was asked to co-produce the library's first video, he brought together old Wellfleetians and new immigrants, encouraging them to talk together without rancor. The forty-minute film was titled *The Wash-Ashores*, thus giving the phrase a permanent place in Cape Cod's vocabulary.

Our foray into small-town politics had convinced us of something we had long suspected—that it was not necessary to depend on ukases from above. A group of determined people could arrive at correct decisions and put them into practice. In other words, democracy worked, although it was often slower that in the old Party days, when our line could change overnight.

After our victory we retreated from town politics. Some of our young friends found the new restrictions onerous and moved to Maine or Nova Scotia seeking greater freedom. But the changed demography brought us other companions. Mike and Ann Ehrenberg, Winnie and Cecil Lubell, and Henry and Dorothy Wright bought or built homes in Wellfleet. We no longer lived close enough to borrow a cup of sugar if unexpected company arrived, but we made up a friendly social nucleus. The men organized a reading group that met monthly to discuss weighty tomes by Friedrich Engels and James Joyce and drove to Orleans on Tuesdays for a game of candlepins. While Ann and Dorothy joined the Friends of the Wellfleet Library and the League of Women Voters, Winnie and I brought together women who wanted to read feminist history and theory. At first some of the women we invited said doubtfully, "I'll have to ask my husband," but we eventually found a hard core of readers who plowed through the writings of Mary Wollstonecraft, Virginia Woolf, and such American commentators as Gerda Lerner, Nancy Cott, Adrienne Rich, and Carolyn Heilbrun. The membership of the group has turned over many times in the last decades; we still meet, but we even read novels and books by men.

From its early days I had cheered the new women's movement without ever finding my own place in it. Betty Friedan's *The Feminine Mystique* had had a bombshell effect on many of my Westchester neighbors, who suddenly felt they had been wasting their lives, but since I had never subscribed to the mystique it did not change my life. I was too old to join the consciousness-raising groups that Anne and her contemporaries formed, so that my first acknowledgment of women's lib was to change my name from "Mrs. Philip Sterling" to "Dorothy Sterling" on all charge accounts and mailing lists. Even that took some doing, as clerks and secretaries insisted on the masculine appellation. I remember the astonishment of a young gynecologist when I asked why he called me "Dorothy" and Phil, "Mr. Sterling," and the bewilderment of a well-intentioned friend when I tried to explain what was wrong with a letter addressed to me as "Ms. Philip Sterling."

In Wellfleet, I subscribed to *Ms.*, became a charter member of the Lower Cape chapter of NOW, and marched in a Fourth of July parade with a contingent of younger women to demand the passage of the Equal Rights Amendment. I was still feeling belligerent about retaining my own name when the Wellesley Class of 1934 invited me to a fortieth reunion. The invitation was addressed to "Mrs. Philip Sterling." After I dashed off a scorching rebuke, the chairman of the program committee telephoned. Would I give a talk on women's liberation at the reunion?

Although I had not been in touch with any Wellesley classmates since I left the college in 1932, I saw this as an opportunity to speak for feminism. Moreover, the invitation had been accompanied by

"1934 in 1974," a report from members of the class telling about their lives. I went through it, calculator in hand and indignation mounting. Out of the class of four hundred who had received superior educations at the height of the Depression, there were only five doctors, two lawyers, one psychologist, one political scientist, one herpetologist. No poets, no novelists, no professors, no artists except hobbyists, and of course no bankers, politicians, or engineers. A fair number were teachers, social workers, nurses, librarians—the traditional women's occupations—but the great majority had never worked outside their homes except briefly before marriage. Instead they had married doctors and bankers and engineers, producing some six hundred children and five hundred grandchildren. "My family has been my main interest," several wrote. "My occupation is taking care of my children," said others.

Booklet in hand, I wrote a statistical analysis of our class's contribution to the world, ending with the hope that our daughters and granddaughters would discover their creative as well as procreative potential. Phil shook his head when he read a draft, and even Anne thought I was too hard on my classmates. But in those first days of fervid feminism I was so sure that I was right that I refused to alter a word.

I was sure that I was right until I walked into the banquet hall and saw the gray haired, pleasant looking sixtyish women who filled the room. Suddenly I realized that I was about to tell them that they had wasted their lives. I picked at my chicken, gulped glasses of water, and dreaded my turn. I read the speech rapidly and sat down to almost complete silence. Afterward a few women came over to say "Interesting speech"; most avoided even making eye contact. Phil and I left quickly. On the way home I scolded myself. Yes, Sisterhood was Powerful, but it should not be smug or unkind.

Shortly after the Wellesley debacle, Florence Howe of the Feminist Press got in touch with me. Founded in 1970, the press's goal was to change the sexist education offered in schools and to encourage Women's Studies as an academic discipline. Florence had just received a grant to develop "Women's Lives/Women's Work," a series for senior high school and college classrooms. Would I contribute to the series with biographies of three black women?

For *Black Foremothers: Three Lives* I chose to tell the stories of Ellen Craft, Mary Church Terrell, and Ida Wells-Barnett. Reporting Ellen Craft's life from a feminist viewpoint proved a challenge because in previous accounts she had been overshadowed by her husband, William. The two had escaped from slavery in Georgia with light-skinned Ellen posing as a planter's son and William as her servant. Once in the North and in England, where they went to escape the slave catchers,

William did all the talking before abolitionist audiences and wrote a best-selling narrative of their escape. Even the report on Ellen in *Notable American Women*, a new biographical dictionary prepared under the auspices of Radcliffe College, said, "As William Craft moved into greater prominence, his wife faded somewhat from view." However, as I searched for contemporary newspaper interviews and letters I found not only that Ellen had borne the brunt of their escape to freedom, but that when they returned to Georgia after the Civil War she ran a school for freedpeople and fought off Klan attacks while William remained in the North raising funds.

Uncovering Ellen Craft's role, which had hitherto been depicted as minor, was my first lesson in feminist historiography. Mary Church Terrell and Ida Wells-Barnett proved easier to write about because both were recognized as women of achievement. My account of Terrell's life was an elaboration of the sketch I had written for the Zenith series, with new material from the diaries that her daughter loaned me. Researching the life of Ida Wells-Barnett was the most interesting. Born of slave parents, she had become a journalist and had led an anti-lynching campaign in the 1890s, daring to write what her male contemporaries feared to say—that the wave of lynchings was not a response to black rapists but part of the campaign to deprive blacks of their newly won rights. Driven from the South by a mob who wrecked her newspaper, she lectured in England, then settled in Chicago, where she continued to work for racial justice after her marriage and the birth of four children. She was in her fifties when she wrote a stirring account of hate-driven riots in East St. Louis, and in her sixties when she traveled to Arkansas in disguise to save the lives of sharecroppers sentenced to death as "black revolutionaries" because they had organized a union.

Phil accompanied me to Chicago, where I talked at length with Alfreda Duster, Wells-Barnett's daughter, and read her papers at the university library. I longed to go on to do a full-length study, until Mrs. Duster told me of two black women who had recently interviewed her about her mother's life. When I returned home a third woman telephoned to say that she planned to write about Wells-Barnett. We swapped information about sources amicably enough until she burst out: "How come Feminist Press asked *you* to write the story of one of *my* people?" I completed *Black Foremothers* but dropped the idea of a longer book. Although I did not then and do not now believe that only black people can write about black people, I was unwilling to compete against younger black women who lacked my experience and contact with publishers. Today I look back on this incident with some regret, because I think I could have written an exciting biography and had a lot of fun doing it. But in the

1970s at the height of the Black Power movement when I was arguing for the right of black people to speak for themselves I could not have done other than I did.

If I had any lingering doubts about this decision, they were dispelled when I went to New York for the 1979 convention of the Association for the Study of Afro-American Life and History. It was the first time I had attended a meeting of the organization since the controversy over the Nat Turner book. This time there were scarcely any white faces at the sessions and, save for Dorothy Porter and her husband Charles Wesley, no one asked me to sit with them. Instead, when a group met to organize the Association of Black Women Historians, its chairman, Rosalyn Terborg-Penn, pointedly asked me not to attend. The incident was a sharp reminder that the days of "Black and White Together/We Shall Overcome" were over. I left the convention a day early.

Although no in-depth biography of Ida Wells-Barnett appeared until 2002, Miriam De Costa-Willis, professor of African-American Studies at the University of Maryland, published Wells' 1885 diary and asked me to write an afterword based on my interviews with Alfreda Duster. Her scholarly study, *The Memphis Diary of Ida B. Wells*, with a foreword by Mary Helen Washington and my afterword, was published by Beacon Press in 1995.

Close to My Heart

By the time I completed *Black Foremothers* I had begun to sample a thirty-volume collection of interviews with ex-slaves that Greenwood Press was bringing out. The interviews had been conducted by WPA writers in the 1930s but had been overlooked until recently. Now, although a half-dozen books had drawn on the material, almost every slave considered had been male. Acting on a hunch, I went to the Boston Public Library with a purse full of dimes. Standing at the Xerox machine day after day, I copied all of the interviews with women—more than a thousand. Reading them at home was a thrilling experience. Here was the real history of slavery as told by mothers, wives, daughters— a portrait of their lives that differed from the accounts by men.

In addition to the WPA interviews, the file boxes stacked on my study floor were overflowing with first-person accounts, letters, and newspaper stories by and about washerwomen, sharecroppers, schoolmarms, doctors that I had been squirreling away for years. Fortunately, I had found a sympathetic editor. After Doubleday let *The Outer Lands* go out of print, James L. Mairs, a vice-president and editor at W. W. Norton, had telephoned to ask if Norton could reprint the book. When he wanted someone to write an introduction, I suggested Robert Finch, a young naturalist who was writing a column for *The Cape Codder*. I also called Jim's attention to *The Run*, John Hay's classic study of a Cape Cod herring run that Doubleday had dropped. Since then Norton has published more than a dozen books by Robert Finch, John Hay, and other Cape Cod nature writers, and I was once again in touch with the New York publishing world.

Jim was interested in history as well as natural history. When Dorothy Porter recently told me that Rayford Logan, the distinguished historian who was collaborating with Michael Winston on a monumental *Dictionary of American Negro Biography*, could not find a publisher, I brought the book to Jim's attention. In preparation for many years—both Phil and I had contributed biographical sketches—the dictionary had several strikes against it. Bad enough that the 800,000-word manuscript would be expensive to produce at a time when interest in black books was waning, but Logan insisted on retaining "Negro" in its title. He had fought for integration all his life and believed that names like "Black" and "Afro-American" implied separatism. Although other publishers had rejected the book because of this, Jim respected Logan's wishes. *The Dictionary of American Negro Biography* was published by Norton in 1982, shortly after Logan's death. Meanwhile I went through a mountain of documents on black women, whittling a thousand-page manuscript down to five hundred pages, and adding dozens of contemporary illustrations. *We Are Your Sisters*—the title taken from a poem

by a black woman—was published in 1984. This was
my first book aimed at adult readers, and I braced
myself for attack. A reviewer in the *San Francisco
Chronicle* asked, in effect, how I could write about
slavery when I am white. Besides, she thought the
book too feminist. A long review in *Women's Review of
Books* by Rosalyn Terborg-Penn said I was not feminist enough but that I had written from "an integra-
tionist viewpoint," focussing on black women as
victims. The latter was so patently untrue that I was
relieved to find a long letter from Mary Helen
Washington in the next issue of *Women's Review*. Then
a professor at Boston College and editor of anthologies of black women's writings, Mary Helen wrote
that while reading *Sisters* she felt "triumphant, elated,
amazed, and at times sorrowful over the incredible
history of my foremothers."

The book is now read in African American and
Women's Studies courses, and the slavery section,
adapted for the stage, is produced in schools and colleges. Nevertheless, I decided that it would be my last
book on black history. The decision was not made just
because of the hostility I had encountered, but because
my voice was no longer needed. So many African
Americans were attending college and graduate programs or beginning careers in journalism that it was
time for me to retire. Along with Martin Luther King, I
still dreamed that some day people would not be

judged by the color of their skin, but that day was far-
ther in the future than anyone had anticipated.

Long before *We Are Your Sisters* was in print, my life
had changed in many ways. Both my parents died,
Dad almost ninety and Mother at eighty-eight. "Our
family is getting shorter," grandson Daniel said. After
all the proper things had been done, I returned to the
Cape, feeling sad, of course, but also shaken to realize
that I was now the older generation, the next in line for
illness and death. I was at the Cape Cod Five Cents
Savings Bank—such a confidence-inspiring name—
arranging to rent a safe deposit box in which to keep
the securities my parents had left me, when a small boy
pointed a finger at me and shouted, "You're old!" How
did he know? How could he tell? I hurried home to
look in the mirror and take stock. Sure enough, there
were silver threads among the gold, and wrinkles,
more wrinkles than I had had freckles as a child.
Nevertheless, I didn't feel old. I still awakened in the
morning thinking of all the good things I would do that
day. I walked the dog, swam and gardened in the summers, and cooked passable meals for Phil and friends.
Although I no longer kept to an eight-hour work day, I
was usually at my desk fighting off interruptions for
five or six hours.

However, I could not easily ignore this new image
of myself. Good Uncle Sam was sending me a Social
Security check each month, and the cashier in the gro-

cery store and the ticket-taker at the movie theater automatically gave me senior discounts. Bad things could happen and sometimes did. Mike Ehrenberg, who was the same age as Phil, died suddenly of a heart attack, leaving a big hole in our small circle. Then Peter and Ellen divorced and their children, Emily and Daniel, joined the army of youngsters who trudged, packs on their backs, to Mom's house one week, Dad's the next. At Christmas, where fifteen members of our extended family had gathered in our living room a year earlier, there were now only seven. Our family had indeed decreased.

Before I had read the galleys of *We Are Your Sisters*, I was at work on a new book, a biography of Abby Kelley, a Quaker who in 1836 had left her teaching job because she felt a "call" to speak against slavery. Breaking with the tradition that condemned women to silence and passivity, she traveled throughout the North, preaching against slavery and inviting women to join the struggle. Married to Stephen Foster, an abo- litionist even more radical that she, she defied custom by continuing to lecture and organize after the birth of their daughter.

Abby Kelley was an ideal subject for me — a woman of commitment who believed that the structure of American society had to be changed in order to root out both white and male supremacy. She was also rigid and doctrinaire in ways that were familiar from the left movement of my day. But save for *Black Foremothers*, I had not really *written* a book for decades. My recent output consisted of collections of documents linked by editorial comment. Besides, this book would be intended for scholars, not young readers. They would expect solid research, footnotes, and bibliography. Could I do it? Some days I felt as if I were still a *Life* researcher who looked on writing as a male prerogative.

But the research was so rewarding that I gradually forgot my fears. Unlike the black people I had written about, Abby Kelley had left a rich paper trail. There were hundreds of letters to and from her in manuscript collections and thousands of references in the antislavery press. Phil spent a week with me in Worcester, where she and her husband had lived and the bulk of her correspondence was stored. We also went to Providence to tour the Moses Brown School, which Abby had attended in 1826, and to go through the Quaker archives in the Rhode Island Historical Society. But as I made plans to visit the libraries in Philadelphia and Washington and to investigate the resources in Boston, Phil began to drag his feet. Slowed by emphysema, he no longer wanted to accompany me on my travels—nor did he want to stay home alone.

A solution was easily found. I no longer needed to travel. Several years earlier, Peter's closest college friend had quit his job as a history professor to join a commune in Oregon. Divesting himself of all his worldly goods, he offered me his microfilm reader, which was considerably better than the small one I had been using. For a $125 check made out to the Bhagwan Rajneesh, I could read microfilm copies of Abby Kelley's letters from a dozen different repositories. I was also able to go through antislavery weeklies—*The Liberator*, *National Anti-Slavery Standard*, and *AntiSlavery Bugle*, an Ohio paper that Abby helped found—and to scan *The Woman's Journal* for the post-Civil War period. Getting to know the day-by-day workings of the antislavery world was fascinating, providing many parallels to politics of the present day. It was also backbreaking, eye-straining, and slow.

Although Phil continued to go bowling on Tuesdays and to write book reports for the men's reading group, his colds had an alarming tendency to develop into bronchitis. A chronic cough led to a chest X-ray, which led to the discovery of a spot on his lung. Was it or wasn't it? A CAT scan said that it was, and Phil went to Brigham and Women's Hospital in Boston for its removal. The post-surgical report sounded like one of those be-glad-you-have-cancer jokes. The tumor had been small and slow-growing—"somnolent," the surgeon characterized it—and he felt sure that it had all been removed.

Phil returned home for a happy occasion—Peter's marriage to Sally Zigmond, a University of

Pennsylvania biologist who shared his enthusiasm for hiking and wind-surfing. On the surface, our lives continued as usual. I was writing Abby Kelley's biography now, struggling to make her come alive and at the same time making sure that all facts were accurate. But we both felt an undercurrent of anxiety, which peaked when it was time for Phil's quarterly X-ray, then eased when his lung was clear. In May 1987, we drove to Westchester for a fiftieth anniversary party at Alice and Leonard's. Two months later family and friends convened in Wellfleet to celebrate Phil's eightieth birthday.

And so another year went by. The feeling of impending doom was never mentioned. I have heard of Anglo-Saxon reserve, but why two Jews refrained from speaking of the topic that most concerned them, I don't understand. We maintained our stiff upper lips even when the quarterly X-ray showed a new tumor. During an endless day, a team of oncologists at Dana Farber Cancer Center went over Phil's records. Since the tumor was slow-growing and causing no symptoms, they advised against surgery or other treatment. Phil was so relieved to hear that he would not be hospitalized that he failed to note that the doctors were really saying, *there's nothing more to be done.* Or perhaps he realized it but did not mention it.

We continued for almost another year, drawn closer by the words unsaid and still unable to breach our reserve. Peter and Anne, who had joined the conspiracy of silence, arranged a fine family vacation on the island of Antigua in the winter of 1989. Peter and Sally wind-surfed and Anne and I snorkeled while Phil sat in the shade of a palm tree, observing. His turn came at dinner, where we joined other friends and he was his usual witty, talkative self. It was one of our better winter vacations.

Back in Wellfleet I finished the first draft of the Abby Kelley biography. Phil, who had provided incisive editorial comments on my previous books, read half of it, but his heart clearly was not in it. He spent more time alone at his desk, sometimes writing poems, which Cecil Lubell published in his poetry column in *The Cape Codder*; at others, working on sketches that he was not ready to discuss.

Spring passed. Summer brought its usual rush of visitors. Then, in August, during one of Phil's regular checkups, the doctor pulled me aside to whisper, "I think there's liver cancer." A day later he phoned to say that a blood test had confirmed the diagnosis. Peter, who was vacationing in Wellfleet, joined me in breaking the news. "I suppose that means another operation," Phil said. "No," I gently replied. The three of us held hands while he tried to take it in. The Hospice people and the books on death—there was one on Phil's bureau—all encouraged the dying person to express his feelings. I tried. Phil tried. Once he said, "I can't imagine what it's like not to exist," and dropped the subject. In the next days, he went downhill, gradually drifting into a coma. Peter, Anne and, Nelson took turns spelling me at night until on September 11, 1989, my partner of a lifetime died in his sleep.

CHAPTER

15

I sleepwalked through the next days, letting others take charge. Leonard took me to our lawyer; Alice wrote Phil's obituary for the *New York Times*; Peter and Anne organized a memorial meeting in our living room. Then I was alone.

I had little time to grieve; fate had other plans in store for me that year. A fortnight after Phil's death I was driving home from the post office when the horizon suddenly tilted, rose to meet the sun, and then tipped sideways again. A day later I was in Massachusetts Eye and Ear Infirmary for an operation on a detached retina. I returned there in November for a second operation and again in May when a hole developed in the macula. Meanwhile I continued to revise the Abby Kelley manuscript, walked the dog, and dined occasionally with friends. The one fixed moment in my routine was the daily phone call from Alice.

Until the day that she did not call. Leonard phoned in her stead to tell me that she was in New York Hospital awaiting surgery to remove a tumor from her lung. I went to New York to take care of her when she returned home, but she remained there only two days. She had developed a raging infection that no antibiotic could cure. For another week Leonard, Ellen, and I sat by her bed, squeezing her hands through a tangle of tubes until she died on April 25, 1990, leaving me doubly bereaved.

During a strange, numb summer I worked on my manuscript in the mornings and swam and gardened in the afternoons. That September I returned to Massachusetts Eye and Ear for a fourth operation. When I awakened from the anaesthetic, Anne had the unpleasant task of telling me that the retina had crumbled in the surgeon's hands. My left eye no longer functioned.

The shape of my days changed. Reading had always been my strategy for coping with anxiety. During stressful periods in the past I had willed time to pass by submerging myself in a book. Now I could only read slowly, maneuvering the book around so as to catch the best light. I could not read to forget my problems because reading *was* my problem. I was afraid that I was going blind.

I did not confide this to anyone. Of course. "Our Crowd" on the Lower Cape—Jews, Christians, atheists—were as reserved with each other as Phil and I had been. The rule was "Don't bellyache," and people seldom did. I certainly did not tell my children that I walked from bedroom to bathroom to kitchen with my eyes closed and arms extended, practicing how to navigate if/when I was blind.

I tried different ways of dealing with my fears. Phil had enjoyed playing with words. I imitated him by keeping a little notebook in which I jotted down phrases like "Cast your eye over this," "You're in a blind alley," "She's the apple of my eye." I considered stealing a BLIND DRIVE sign from the road, adding an "R" and attaching it to my rear license plate. When I mentioned this to a passenger in my car, she blanched. Jokes were not much help if those you shared them with thought them macabre.

Nor did I confide to anyone that there were many hours in the day when I stretched out on my bed and listened to tape-recorded books. I started with thrillers like Clancy's *The Hunt For Red October* or *Tinker, Tailor, Soldier, Spy* by John Le Carré, but my conscience bothered me. Alice and I had strict rules about watching television or reading novels during the day. No soap operas or sitcoms for us. I had confined my daytime reading to pertinent history or biography. So now I began to fill in the gaps in my education with the *Iliad*, the *Odyssey*, and *Moby-Dick*. I had long ago taught myself speed reading, selecting the salient points in a paragraph, then going on to the next. This system of scanning and skipping did not work when reading by ear. If I missed sentences I had to push the rewind

button and start over again, a time-consuming procedure that often put me to sleep. Instead of hearing
Homer's measured cadences I dozed for a large part of
each afternoon.

More practically, I also began attending the monthly
meetings of a Sight Loss group at Wellfleet's Senior
Center. Of the dozen or so people who gathered there,
everyone's vision was worse than mine. Yet no one
thought it ironic to greet a member with "So glad to see
you" or "How well you are looking." Everyone laughed
with the one totally blind member of the group when he
told of his wife leaving him a note to say where she had
gone—and laughed again when a woman who wore a
peaked cap to hide her scarred eyes said, "Disabled!
We're not disabled, we just can't see."

The leader of the group, a cheerful, capable woman
who navigated with the help of a Seeing-Eye dog, put
me in touch with the National Library Service for the
Blind, which sent catalogues listing tens of thousands
of books on tape. Not only could I research new topics,
but I could listen to such periodicals as *Playboy*. I never
discovered how the Librarian of Congress brought the
Playboy bunnies to life for sightless readers because I
was also introduced to a low-vision specialist who
helped install a strip of halogen lights on my kitchen
ceiling, a gooseneck halogen lamp next to my favorite
living room chair, and a small, powerful light on the
wall above my bed. Once again I could read the news-

paper at breakfast and tackle any book I chose the rest of the day. The tape recorder was stored in a bureau drawer, and I stopped sleeping the afternoons away.

There was still work to be done on the book. I found a portrait of Abby Kelley for the cover and settled on a title: *Ahead of Her Time: Abby Kelley and the Politics of Antislavery.* I wrote an introduction and dedication—to Phil and Alice—and rechecked the footnotes and bibliography. By the time everything had been shipped to New York I was sometimes putting in eight-hour days, to my amazement and exhilaration.

Around this time I had an unusual dream. Heretofore my dreams had been anxiety-driven. I was going on a trip but had forgotten my passport, lost my suitcase, missed my plane. This dream was different. I had had a baby, but had come home leaving her behind in the hospital. A nurse called, asking why I did not come to see her. She was really a lovely baby, the nurse said. In response to her urging I went to the hospital, but instead of visiting the baby I read a magazine and talked with another new mother.

The dream made such an impression that I recounted it to Anne the next day. "Mom," my wise daughter said, "Modern dream therapists believe the person you're dreaming about is you. You are the new baby."

This certainly gave me something to think about. For two years I had been attempting to carry on in my same old way, despite the many changes that had taken place. A major change was Anne. Shortly before Phil's death, she had told us that her twenty-year marriage to Nelson was breaking up. In the emotional turmoil of Phil's last weeks I had not thought about this often. It was only afterward that I realized that the break had come because she wanted to live with another woman. She soon met Paula Vogel, a professor at Brown and a brilliant young playwright who was also warm, witty, and caring. I love and respect my daughter very much and, although I missed Nelson, I feel fortunate to have Paula as a member of my extended family.

Then other good things began to happen. The History Book Club chose *Ahead of Her Time* as a monthly selection, the Book-of-the-Month Club offered it as an alternate, and Eric Foner, professor of history at Columbia, gave it a long, favorable review in the *New York Times*. After forty years as a children's book author, I was being taken seriously as a historian. When the publication of the Abby Kelley biography coincided with my seventy-eighth birthday, friends gave me a party. Our artist host made a collage for the occasion. It showed a knight on horseback, with my face superimposed, one hand holding a pen instead of a sword, the other a copy of *Ahead of Her Time*.

This collage marked the final turning point for me. Surrounding myself with cartons of clippings and let-ters, I began to work on this memoir. Much of the cor-

respondence was Phil's—he had been a paper-saver—
but I was surprised to discover school magazines from
Spec Op and Dalton and some college themes that
helped me to recall, often with embarrassment, what I
had been thinking about in the 20s and 30s. I did not
know if I could write a coherent story or if anyone
would care to read it, but I slowly began organizing the
material.

While I was examining the past I was overwhelmed by the staggering changes in Eastern
Europe. On Alice's last visit to the Cape we had
watched the dismantling of the Berlin Wall on television. Although she had scarcely thought about Karl
Marx since her Vassar YCL days, she asked in bewilderment, "Is it possible that socialism does not work?"
I pondered the question again as more walls came
tumbling down and newspapers ran such headlines as
"SOVIETS BAR COMMUNISTS PARTY ACTIVITIES" and
"SOVIET UNION TO DISSOLVE." Whenever old left-
wingers got together—not only communists but
fellow travelers, socialists, even Trotskyists who now
spoke with their former enemies—we asked the same
questions. What had gone wrong? When should we
have known? Was socialism really dead? We had been
separated from the movement for decades, but sparks
of our youthful idealism still flickered. It was painful
to watch the destruction of everything we had once
believed in.

Steve Nelson became my most frequent visitor. Steve had fought for the Loyalists in Spain and had been a member of the Central Committee of the U.S. Party. He had resigned the day after Khrushchev's revelations about Stalin became public and had earned his living as a carpenter until his retirement to Truro in the 1970s. We became close friends after the deaths of Phil and of Steve's wife, Margaret. Although he freely admitted to the mistakes the Party had made, he was an unquenchable optimist who brought me daily reports on world politics. When there was little good news in the papers he told gripping stories of the Spanish War or of his confinement in a Pennsylvania prison, where he was jailed for sedition during the 50s.

Steve was a remarkable storyteller and a remarkable man. He welded a chain of people on the Lower Cape who he called "The Family": members of the men's reading and bowling groups to which Phil had belonged, founders of a new peace group, young people who wanted to learn about the past, and old-timers like me who liked to talk about it. He felt responsible for us all, gently scolding if someone seemed in danger of going astray, comforting those who were unhappy, binding us all together with his love and concern. He rarely came to visit without beans from his garden, a pot of homemade soup, a jar of Truro cranberries. Even when I invited him for dinner he insisted on bringing the sauce for the spaghetti or a pie he had baked. Perhaps socialism did not work, but Steve was close to my ideal of Socialist Man. When he died in 1993, just before his ninetieth birthday, it was a grievous loss for many of us.

In the first years after Phil's death, I continued to travel, but noisy airports and long plane trips proved tiring, and I now go over the bridge, as Cape Codders say, only for special occasions. One of these took place in 1994, when Harvard's Department of Afro-American Studies and its W. E. B. Du Bois Institute wanted to give a party to mark the end of the academic year and called it "A celebration of the lives and works of Dorothy Porter and Dorothy Sterling." Dorothy and I occupied the places of honor at a reception and dinner; it was our last time together. The second trip came a year later, when Brown University awarded me the degree of Doctor of Humane Letters. Describing me as "a self-taught historian," the citation said that "at a time when many refused to recognize the omissions that marred the teaching of American history," I had introduced young people to the facts of the past by "chronicling the lives of African Americans, abolitionists and women with meticulous scholarship and nuanced commentary." The recognition was flattering, because my companions on the platform included such well known figures as Shimon Peres, then Israel's minister of foreign affairs, Maya Lin, the youthful designer of the Vietnam Veterans Memorial in Washington, and

South African playwright Athol Fugard. I returned home with a handsome red and black satin hood, which I will wear as a shawl when I am really old.

Now I punctuate my days with trips to the post office and library. When Karl Marx—or was it Engels?—wrote of "the idiocy of the village" he could not have foreseen Wellfleet. Few villages with a winter population hovering around three thousand have two Greek study groups as well as library seminars whose topics range from the origin of fairy tales to Joyce's *Ulysses*. Or a summer theater that eschews old musical comedies in favor of plays by Mamet, Fugard, and Paula Vogel. Or a board of selectmen whose members have included a popular novelist and a retiree from the State Department. Or a police chief who writes mystery stories in his free time. At the post office I exchange greetings with a 60s radical who is now a skilled cabinet maker, with the plumber who mopped my basement floor when the washing machine overflowed—surely a violation of the plumbing code—or the librarian who procures new books for me through inter-library loan, via a program titled CLAMS. Even strangers greet me to comment on an unusually high tide or to tell of a fox glimpsed crossing the road. It's the kind of small town friendliness that I had dreamed of but never found in Rye.

But is this enough? Not quite. I have bought a computer on which I am typing this final chapter. I send e-mail messages to friends and grandchildren and plan to listen to chat groups on the Internet when I have time. But I still spend many hours reading in an effort to make sense out of the eight decades I have witnessed. I continue to be overwhelmed by new disclosures about the past. Steve Nelson once hypothesized that the path of socialism might have been different had Lenin survived. Now I read that Lenin was almost as great a monster as Stalin. Furthermore, Julius Rosenberg *was* a spy, and the American Communist Party did receive millions of dollars of Moscow gold each year, just as its enemies said. (Why then did we hold those interminable Saturday night fundraisers?) I know more than I care to about the love lives of Franklin D. Roosevelt and John Kennedy. I wince when I read that Thurgood Marshall was an FBI informer, and that even saintly Albert Einstein was a male chauvinist pig who—is it possible?—had an affair with a Soviet spy.

Despite these proofs of my naivete, I cannot overcome the belief that many of the things we worked for have made life better for ordinary people. The tender warriors I met in the 1950s will never again see a WHITES ONLY sign. The first black girl to enter the University of Georgia became a television commentator. One of the Little Rock Nine served as an assistant secretary of state. Orial Redd's daughter, once judged unfit to live in a "white" apartment house, is now a

Westchester County executive with 31,000 employees under her jurisdiction.

Forty years after my disastrous attempt to introduce Negro History Week in Rye's elementary school, African-American History month is celebrated all over the country. The Dick and Jane primers have been consigned to the dust bin, and books reporting on the struggles and achievements of black people are available from pre-school to college. Once Langston Hughes could not earn a living as a writer. Now black authors make the best-seller lists and Toni Morrisson has been awarded the Nobel prize.

The recognition of the role of African-Americans has spilled over to encompass other minorities. Schools now tentatively teach that Columbus did *not* discover America; on Thanksgiving Day Native Americans travel to Plymouth Rock for a National Day of Mourning. Indulgent parents can buy African-American, Hispanic, and Asian versions of Barbie dolls.

And so it goes in other fields close to my heart. Despite glass ceilings, sexual harassment, and inadequate child care, women have become doctors, lawyers, college presidents. They sit in Congress, on the Supreme Court, in the Cabinet. No public school requires girls to take sewing while the boys study science; the Harvard Club long ago closed its Ladies entrance.

I check off the items on my balance sheet. The genie that Harry Truman uncorked at Hiroshima has started conflagrations around the world, threatening the very existence of humankind. But there are bright spots, too. The poisoning of the earth with pesticides has stopped in many places. Thanks to increased awareness of the environment, Wellfleet's trees are no longer sprayed with pesticides each spring, and the marsh in front of my house is now owned by the Conservation Trust.

BUT, but, but. In the inner cities infants die at twice the rate of those in the suburbs. Children are cut down in a crossfire between rival drug dealers; children kill children, and the NRA successfully lobbies against laws to control guns. All over the world, as the free market triumphs over planned economies, there is a growing disparity between rich and poor. With profit the sole motive, America's economy prospers, while child laborers work in sweatshops in Asia to supply sneakers for U.S. mall walkers. "Greed is good!" intones a character in a movie.

I no longer have glib solutions to these problems. The slogans we shouted when we paraded through the streets asking for equality and justice for all were simplistic, but they had a nobility about them that is lacking today. As the World's Oldest Living Bolshevik says in Tony Kushner's *Perestroika*, "You who live in this Sour Little Age cannot imagine the grandeur of the

prospect we gazed upon; like standing on the highest
peak in the mighty Caucasus, and viewing in one all-
knowing glance the mountainous, granite order of cre-
ation. You cannot imagine it. . . . What have you to
offer in its place?"

EPILOGUE

My larger story ends around 1993 with the final col-
lapse of my generation's inspired vision of world
socialism. But the smaller drama of my own life has
continued. I have suffered more losses of the kind one
must expect after eighty; yet I have also experienced
significant pleasures, which, for being unexpected, are
all the greater. And there appeared one more windmill
that demanded a tilt—which I made—with a deeply
satisfying result.

The losses include the deaths, now with accelerat-
ing pace, of many beloved friends and companions.
Robert Riley, with whom I shopped and dined and
schmoozed many an evening over the last decade, is
gone. Leonard Lake, my brother-in-law, with whom I
shared an abiding affection for my sister and then a
deep mutual affection, is gone. Alan Woodle, the
builder of our utopian house in Rye, called regularly
from Alabama until neither of us could any longer hear
on the telephone. Then we e-mailed, but now he is

gone. And so are Dave and Rosemarie Scherman, Cecil Lubell, Stanley Robbins, and Anna DeCormis.

Yet I remain blessed with Hilda and Herb Lass, Anne Ehrenberg, and Winnie Lubell—with whom I still visit regularly. Their friendships of seven decades can not be overvalued. And over my thirty years in Wellfleet, I have accumulated a host of "new" friends, both native and "wash-a-shore." Not to forget my children, who call and visit regularly. They give thoughtful advice, which is usually reliable, though often just a little before I am ready to consider it.

I have survived to witness my grandchildren mature and follow the family callings. Daniel is now a successful comedy writer in Los Angeles with an eye for social satire—which Phil would have loved, while also worrying about how Hollywood might affect his soul. Emily became a social worker, doing AIDS outreach, psychotherapy, and community support in poor, Hispanic neighborhoods of Philadelphia and Boston, putting her fluent Spanish to a use that her grandfather would have equally approved. Keeping the apples close, Emily married William Graves, who served in the Peace Corps in Africa and is now an immigration lawyer who travels from Boston to New Hampshire to visit poor clients in the INS hoosegow. Together they have produced Sam—middle name, Philip, for his great-grandfather. At four Sam is sunny, articulate, and affectionate; what is more, he can tell a jay from a cardinal by the call. And now there is Rebecca, eight months as I write, and crawling about in search of fresh detritus to taste. These events in the "gains" column help make bearable the loss of my companions.

Fourteen years have passed since Phil died, and now at ninety I live alone overlooking a beach that in winter is raked by wind and tide-borne ice. Afflicted with chronic obstructive pulmonary disease, the medical profession's euphemism for emphysema, I move about the house tethered to a polyvinyl line that silently wafts oxygen to my nostrils. It was discouraging at first and embarrassing, but I have got used to it. And last year my glaucoma doctor operated to protect my rapidly dimming vision—but extinguished it. Thus my worst terror, that I would be blind, has been realized. But, guess what? I have got used to that, too.

Of course, to keep me going takes more or less the village. Emilie and John Doucette, who first cared for the house, now care for me—with rides to the doctor, shopping, laying out my clothes. John has kept my garden going, so I can still enjoy some of my long-term pleasures: a few asparagus in spring, some real tomatoes and basil in the summer. And he has been endlessly inventive at adapting the house to match my failing vision: installing lights strong enough to cook our Christmas goose; distributing telephones to keep me from running for a call—and risk breaking yet another bone. When I finally lost all form vision, John placed a fluorescent beacon over the kitchen doorway to orient me and set up ropes by which I guide myself from bedroom to kitchen. Following the ropes, I can stride thirty laps when bad weather keeps me indoors.

Every morning, Annette Silva, an intelligent and ebullient woman, arrives to help me bathe, set up my lunch and my special 5:00 P.M. treat, an ample shot of bourbon. She returns in the evening to help me prepare for bed and set up my morning coffee. On some days young Autumn Joseph reads me my e-mail and sends my replies. All my tenders help to straighten out my books-on-tape—which have become my prime entertainment. Old friends, plus a gratifying number of acquaintances from the community, come by to read aloud selected articles and book reviews from the *New York Times* and some choice local items from the *Cape Codder*.

Undeniably my sensory world has shrunk, but I manage to inhabit it. In decent weather a neighbor will appear, frequently John Stryker, to shoulder my oxygen tank and guide me over the rutted road for a mile amidst bird calls and in season the fragrance of rugosa rose. When the Graveses drive down from Boston, which they frequently do, Sam's embrace is strong and warm, and Rebecca's skin so soft.

Certainly there are periods of frank boredom, and then I entertain myself by reconstructing scenes from the past. As it turns out, my trait of stubborn independence that was impossible for my mother to love, and so caused me pain, serves me perfectly at this stage when people seem to admire, even cherish it.

The other night, sleeping restlessly, I rolled over on my Med-Alert. This notified an operator, somewhere in the night, who called me. Unfortunately my hearing aid was on the night table, and I failed to answer, so, following the protocol, she called the Wellfleet Fire & Rescue squad, who promptly sent a man to check me out. Of course he had been here before for other late-night misadventures—mainly respiratory attacks—so he felt okay opening the front door and stealing silently in for a peek. When, standing at my bedroom door, he heard me breathing regularly, he crept back out, left a note, and returned to the station. John Doucette, who had also been called, arrived shortly after and did the same. If I can't have world socialism, then a village full of kind and sensible people is very satisfying.

Shellfish wars

Wellfleet harbor empties with the tide, uncovering vast flats that are prime grounds for shellfish. Mainly there are oysters and the hard-shelled clam, named *quahog* by the Wampanoags, who harvested them here for centuries. Testimony to this is a huge shell midden perched on the dune about half a mile from my house, a section long known as Indian Neck. In the 1980s the town initiated a new industry by leasing sections of the Indian Neck flats to local men and women who began to culture the shellfish systematically—laying out seed clams purchased from a breeder in Dennis and encouraging oyster larvae to settle down on old shells and concrete "coolie hats." The shellfish require protection against myriad predators—moon snails, spider crabs, whelks, and gulls—and receiving this they flourish into sweet and briny morsels that provide a full living or significant supplement for dozens of families in the town.

The work is hard: hot in summer, freezing in winter, and the only convenient access is a sand road belonging to the owners of my development. We are a few year-rounders, but mostly summer people whose houses dominate the dunes and look down upon the beach—and on the flats when they become exposed for a few hours at low tide. In 1995 some owners, complaining to the town that the shellfish nets and truck tracks were unsightly and dangerous to swimmers and boaters, tried to block leases from being renewed. This moved me to write a letter to the *Cape Codder*, pointing out that recreational uses occur at high tide when the netting is all hidden safely under water; also the truck tracks are completely obliterated by the incoming tide. I also noted that aquaculture makes sense with Wellfleet's history, is ecologically sound, and adds more than a million dollars annually to the economy.

Yet in 1998, to my astonishment and shame, several owners on the dunes sued the shellfishers, citing colonial law that awarded ownership down to mean low tide. Once more I wrote to the Cape Codder, pointing out that our deeds specifically limit the upland owners to the mean *high water* mark. I took the further step, possibly more important, of inviting the shellfishers to use the private road as my guests. Which they do at every low tide, never failing to repair the broken berm, to neaten up the beach, and to greet interested summer visitors and explain their business.

The case dragged on for several years, bleeding the shellfishers with legal fees—which were inconsequential to my rich neighbors on the dunes. Eventually the shellfishers prevailed in state court. In late summer 2001, the shellfishers held a ceremony, where my road meets the beach, to celebrate my contribution to their victory. There were speeches with donuts and hot coffee—and the cut from road to beach was officially named Sterling Pass. The ceremony ended with the presentation of a handsome granite bench inscribed with a quote from my book *The Outer Lands*. Today the bench faces the harbor a few feet above high water—where I suppose it might remain for another generation—before it is washed over by the rising sea.

DOROTHY STERLING

INDEX